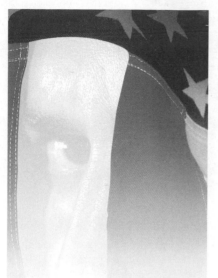

Who Stole the American Dream II ?

Burke Hedges

I N T I

Who Stole the American Dream II?
By Burke Hedges

Printed in the United States of America
First edition, January 1992

ISBN: 1-891279-18-1

Published by INTI, Inc.
Cover design and layout by Parry Design Studio

intipublishing.com

A 'Facts Lift' for a Classic

It's been a long time since the first edition of *Who Stole the American Dream?*—the best selling book in the history of Network Marketing—was first published.

Fifteen years, to be exact.

I wrote the book in the summer and fall of 1991, and it was released to the public in December of that year. Scary to think how many changes I've seen during those 15 years. Off the top of my head, here are a few.

Back in 1991, there was no commercial Internet. No email. No hybrid automobiles. No GPS navigation. No Starbucks outside Seattle. No DVD players. No free long distance. No caller ID. No satellite TV or radio. No flat-screen TVs. No hi-definition TVs. No lightweight laptop computers. No MP3 players. No iPods. No Palm Pilots. No BlackBerries. No X-boxes. No digital cameras or camcorders. No debit cards. And just a few fax machines.

Back in 1991, cell phones were clunky and expensive, service was limited, and features were few: No ring tones. No cameras. No calendars. No games. No phone book. No voice recognition.

Back in 1991, the U.S. exported more than it imported... China and India were third-world economies... the Berlin Wall had just come down... the Soviet Union was just converting to capitalism... gasoline cost $1.04 per gallon... GM was the biggest, most profitable company in the world... the airlines made money... college tuition was still affordable... companies that laid off thousands of workers saw their stock prices fall, instead of rise... Wal-Mart did not sell groceries... Fox TV was a fledgling network... and Iraq invaded Kuwait, sparking the first Gulf War.

Back in 1991, I described the basic premise of my first edition of *Who Stole the American Dream?* with these words: "Somebody—or more accurately, a whole big bunch of somebodies—has stolen the American Dream. Right out from under our hard-working noses."

Sadly, it's still happening today. And this totally revised edition will tell you how to get it back!

Dedication

To my father, Burke O. Hedges, who passed away when I was a child; and to the men and women who dare to take advantage of our greatest right of all—FREE ENTERPRISE!

Also by Burke Hedges

• Who Stole the American Dream?

• You Can't Steal Second with Your Foot on First!

• You, Inc.

• Read & Get Rich

• Copycat Marketing 101

• Dream-Biz.com

• Parable of the Pipeline

Acknowledgments

This book would not have been possible without the relentless support of John Fogg and Steve Price, two dear friends whom I admire enormously.

A special thanks to my five children—Burke, Jr., Nathan, Spencer, Aspen, and Alina—for their continued support in every endeavor I dare to undertake. And to my mother, Maritza, and my stepfather, Harley, for their faith in me.

A big thanks to all of my teammates at INTI Publishing who take care of the homestead while I venture down entrepreneurial paths: Katherine Glover, the Organizer; Debbie Cortes, the Marketer; Tony Cortes, the technician; Steve Price, the thinker; Sandee Lorenzen, the Coordinator; Gail Brown, the Jack of All Trades; Julia Bullough, the Detail Person; and Dianna Bazalar, the Versatile One.

Finally, my gratitude, deep admiration, and love for two people who passed away, darkening my doorstep forever: Ted von Schullick, a co-worker and good friend; and Dayton, a younger brother whom I miss daily.

Contents

Introduction:

Stop, Thief!

I'm a gentleman.
I live by robbing the poor.
—George Bernard Shaw
Irish playwright & social critic

S omething was terribly wrong!
As I slipped my key into the front door
lock, I had a strange, unsettling feeling. I
could feel an almost electric tingling sensation on my arms and hands.
My stomach was suddenly empty... I felt oddly hollow and sick.

I opened the door and cautiously walked inside. It wasn't getting
any better. It actually hurt now.

I looked around. I was in the right house. Nothing was out of
place. It just didn't feel right—and the feeling was getting worse by the
second.

Then I saw it. There was a hole right under the television where
the DVD player used to be. It was gone!

"Oh, no," I thought. "What else did they steal?"

Stop, THIEF!

Somebody had broken into my home, messed around with my
stuff, rifled through and ripped off my private things—and my kids'
things, too—*they'd even stolen from my kids!*

If this has ever happened to you, you'll probably never forget the
feeling. I know I never will. As I remember this incident now, even
though it happened years ago, those uncomfortable physical sensations
return immediately.

It was awful—and it's still awful. I felt—dishonored... personally
violated... angry... and absolutely powerless to do anything about it!

That's how we feel when someone steals from us.

And those are the feelings we have about someone breaking into our home and stealing stuff—just material things, which, in my case, I went out and replaced in less than a week.

Imagine how much more shaken, angry, and powerless we'd feel if someone stole so private and precious a thing as our dreams.

And that's just what they've done.

Somebody—or more accurately, a whole big bunch of some-bodies—has stolen the American Dream. Right out from under our hard-working noses.

We've had our hopes and dreams ripped off, our futures stolen and fenced by a bunch of freewheeling felons getting rich at our expense.

THE AMERICAN DREAM HAS BECOME A MYTH

The American Dream is a fairy tale—

Not because it's not real...

Not because it's a thing of the past...

Not because it's not possible to achieve anymore, either...

And not because we don't deserve it. Absolutely not that!

It's become a myth because the way we've been brought up—and the things we've been taught we had to do to achieve the American Dream—simply don't work anymore.

And what's more, that whole business of "Get a college degree, work your way up the corporate ladder or start your own small business and achieve your dreams..." could be a setup. For an increasing number of us, it's turned into a con, a scam, and a scheme the big-shot power people use to get us to work our lives away trading too much time for not enough money just to make them rich!

Just thinking about it brings up the same feelings in me that I had when my home was broken into... with one exception.

This time I don't feel powerless. Not anymore.

I found a way to get back the American Dream.

But before I tell you my way—the average person's way—let me ask you some questions.

2

WHAT IS THE AMERICAN DREAM?

Is the American Dream going to college and getting a degree? Now, you know that works for some, but really—how many? And isn't it true that for the doctors, lawyers, and Indian chiefs of government and corporate America—the future isn't what it used to be? How many college grads find work in their chosen fields today? How many are doing that same work 10 years later... or even 5 years later? Likely one out of a hundred.

Is the American Dream getting a good job? Working for a living? Can you get a job where you can earn what you're worth... where you'll become financially independent... and find fulfillment... and gain freedom... trading your time for money?

Did you know that over half of all first-time heart attacks occur between the hours of 8 a.m. and 10 a.m. Monday morning? That tells me that *people would rather die than go back to work*!

There's no loyalty in corporate America anymore—and no security, either. GM is laying off 30,000 workers. Ford is shuttering more than a dozen North American factories. China and India are booming and building like a gold-rush town, while the once-major G-8 industrialized nations are steadily edging toward 20% unemployment (the youth in Spain, France, and Germany are already there!).

What about owning your own small business... is that the American Dream? I tried that. Made a million dollars—but it cost me $1.2 million to make it!

Did you know that 90% of all small businesses fail in the first year?... and 80% of the survivors close their doors in the next 5 years?... and 80% of those lucky survivors never see year 10? Which means fewer than 1 out of 100 small businesses last a decade or longer.

Doesn't look like owning a conventional small business is the way to achieve the American Dream, does it?

Now, notice I said, "conventional" business.

THE TIMES WE LIVE IN

We live in unconventional times, which call for unconventional ways of doing things.

New and better and different ways.

3

Ideas that used to take 50 years to be born, grow, and mature—now take only 5 years… or fewer. For example, it took radio 38 years to reach 50 million listeners. It took TV 13 years to reach the 50-million mark. *It only took the Internet 4 years to attract 50 million users!*

Everything's changing—and changing so rapidly that the great success stories of just a few short years ago are outmoded, dying dinosaurs today.

Here's a recent example: VHS recorders.

If you owned a successful business manufacturing VHS recorders or tapes in the 1980s and early '90s, you were probably a very rich person—a millionaire many times over. Where would you be today? *Out of business*! DVDs knocked VCRs right off the shelf of your entertainment center. DVD players take up less space, offer better sound and picture, have more options, and are easier to use.

R.I.P., VHS.

As I write this, DVDs are king of the hill, but change is happening so fast in the electronics industry that China is already busy writing the obituary for DVDs, gearing up to replace them with hi-definition EVDs (Enhanced Versatile Disks). And you better believe there's some techno-nerd in some lab developing the technology that will eventually knock digital technology right out of the ring.

Are you beginning to see the picture?

THE FUTURE IS NOW

Ladies and gentlemen, tomorrow is happening today. If you can't see it, if you don't know what's coming, you're going to be left behind. And not just one or two steps behind either—miles behind! And things are moving so fast you may never catch up—ever!

Look, if you're not already in place, at the top, on a leading-edge career track where your job is out in the margins, literally working in the future today, you've got no better than one chance in 10,000 of making it to the top of an Old Economy company. Believe me, it's true. What's left over are dull, dead-end government jobs, like airport luggage checkers… or cheap, unfulfilling service jobs—cleaning up after or waiting on the hot-shots smart enough to go where the action is now… and, more importantly, where it will be in the future.

Look around you. It's already happening. Leading-edge entrepreneurs, like the founders of MySpace.com, Facebook.com, and YouTube.com, are working in the future by cashing in on the Internet, even after the dot.com bubble burst. The three guys who started YouTube, for example, sold it to Google for $1.65 BILLION only one year after starting the company.

Mind boggling, isn't it? Oh, to be a computer geek....

In Yogi Berra's words, "The future ain't what it used to be."

THE CHANGING AMERICAN WORKPLACE

Do you think "big steel" and other U.S. heavyweight industries are going to make a comeback? Who's going to replace a robot or some other error-free, automated machine that just replaced 20 human beings for less than half the money they were being paid—and that does a better job?

Just try getting a high-paying factory job today in Detroit... Pittsburgh... or Cleveland. There's a reason they call it the "rust belt."

Let's face it, blue-collar jobs are becoming extinct. Think I exaggerate? Ford Motor Company is planning to eliminate 75,000 American jobs and close more than a dozen North American factories by 2012, and they're seriously thinking about terminating three high-end brands—Jaguar, Land Rover, and Lincoln. GM is closing 14 plants and PERMANENTLY ELIMINATING 30,000 jobs in the U.S. and Canada.

Poof—once-secure jobs gone forever. And that's just the beginning.

So, what about white-collar jobs?

I can answer that with one bureaucratic buzz word: *outsourcing*.

The U.S. will lose 6 million high-paid white-collar workers to India in the coming decade. And not just call centers. Entire info-tech departments are being outsourced to India. Along with accounting services. Healthcare services. Banking and back office support. Software design and production. Even movie-making, all in the effort to save money and boost profits for the fat cats at the top and the hedge fund managers who badger CEOs to get "leaner and meaner" in exchange for buying their stock.

5

The rich are getting richer—and the poor...? We all know the answer to that!

Let's see—college degrees, corporate careers, small businesses, blue-collar jobs, white-collar jobs... all heading for underemployment or overseas.

Where can people turn to recapture the American Dream? What's left?

What's left is a way of life and work called Network Marketing—the most powerful form of distribution of goods and services available in the world today. A new and better way of working and living. A proven industry that people from every walk of life are turning to. A way for the average person to achieve the American Dream.

That's what this book is about.

YOU DESERVE TO KNOW THE TRUTH ABOUT NETWORK MARKETING

Networking will be in your future in one of three ways:
- You'll be one of the people who's making it happen; or,
- You'll be one of the people who's watching it happen; or...,
- You'll be one of the people wondering "What happened?"

It's simple. You'll either be one of the millions of ordinary men and women who achieve extraordinary lifestyles through Network Marketing—or you'll be one of those who wish they had.

I guarantee you that by the mid-21st century, if you're not a Network Marketer, you'll be one of those other millions of people throughout North America and the world buying things from them... making things they buy... serving them... or waiting on them.

Bold talk? Yes—the boldest. And yes, I've earned the right.

MY STORY

You see, I had the American Dream stolen from me—just like I'm saying most of you have. I've experienced those feelings in the pit of my stomach: broke, scared, couldn't pay the bills, couldn't provide for the kids, no vacation, no fun, no future—frustrated, angry, and feeling powerless to change it.

Then I discovered Network Marketing. And, yes—perhaps like you—I was skeptical at first. It sounded too good to be true. I felt it was just some sales scam—you know, a pyramid scheme.

But, hey, it didn't cost me anything to check it out—and what if it were true? What if it really was my ticket to the American Dream? I couldn't afford to risk losing out!

They say the mind is like a parachute—it doesn't work unless it's open. So, I opened up my mind. I tucked my doubts and disbelief under my arm and took a look.

What I found was that Network Marketing really was simple— even I, a boat-builder earning $5.50 an hour who couldn't pass the test to become an insurance adjustor, could do it! It was fun, too. There were lots of people to help me. I got to make a powerful, positive difference in hundreds, even thousands, of people's lives. And, yes, I made money, too—more than I ever dreamed possible, in fact!

But who cares what I did? Who cares what I think?

The important question is, "What do you think?"

ONLY YOUR OPINION COUNTS

Is Network Marketing right for you? Can you be successful in Network Marketing—will you?

I don't know the answer to that. But I do know that you absolutely, positively owe it to yourself to learn the truth about Network Marketing.

I mean—what if... ?

What's it going to take for you to learn the truth, the whole truth, and nothing but the truth? The cost of this book and a couple of hours of reading—max.

It will be time and money well and wonderfully spent. That's a promise.

You see, in my opinion, Network Marketing is the wave of the future.

In my opinion, Network Marketing is called "a personal franchise" for a good reason.

In my opinion, Network Marketing is putting the freedom back into free enterprise.

In my opinion, Network Marketing is the very best way in the world—perhaps the only way—for average people like you and me to live far-above-average lives.

But that's my opinion.

In the classic novel, *Fathers and Sons*, Russian author Ivan Turgenev wrote:

"I share no man's opinion. I have my own."

So, it's really your opinion of Network Marketing that counts—isn't it?

See, it doesn't really matter what my opinion is.

You've got to know for yourself, isn't that true?

What really matters is what you think and feel about Network Marketing. In short, you've got to know what's in it for you!

I promise you this: If you'll just take the time to learn about who stole the American Dream—and then determine for yourself if you can get it back with Network Marketing—then you'll know if Network Marketing is the right vehicle for you.

NO EXCUSES

Now I know some of you will make excuses for not investigating this industry. Some people will say, "I don't have the time"... or "It's not for me"... or "I'm too old to try something new"... and so on.

All these half-baked excuses remind me of a guy who wanted to mow his grass, but his mower was broken. So he went next door to his neighbor's house and asked if he could use their lawn mover.

"Sorry," said the neighbor. "I can't lend you my lawn mower because my wife is cooking beef stroganoff."

Startled by his neighbor's response, the man asked, "What does your wife cooking beef stroganoff have to do with you lending me your lawn mower?"

The neighbor looked him square in the eye and replied, "If I don't want to loan you my lawn mower, any excuse will do!"

NOTHING TO LOSE

How about you—are you accepting just any excuse to avoid finding out about this industry? Hey, if you've made all the money you'll ever spend (and you have the time and freedom to enjoy it)… you probably don't need to investigate the possibilities of becoming successful in Network Marketing.

But if you're like most of us, you've got everything to gain and nothing to lose by finding out the facts about this fast-growing industry.

There's no better time to check it out than right now!

And if you decide that Network Marketing is for you, you'll look back on this moment in time as the single most important moment in your life!

This could be that special moment when you start to take control of your life again… the moment you begin to feel the freedom, security, and happiness of the American Dream.

Best of all, it could be the moment you start to make *the* American Dream—*your* American Dream!

The
American
Dream

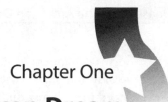

Chapter One

The Myth of the American Dream

America is too great for small dreams.
—Pres. Ronald Reagan

W hat is the American Dream? We all have our own unique version of what the American Dream means. Ask a million people to describe their dreams, and you'll have a million separate, distinct, and uniquely individual pictures. However, there are a number of things that all our dreams have in common, no matter how different each of us is.

We all want freedom and security for ourselves and our families. We want more money than we have now. We want health and happiness. We want to do something meaningful and stimulating. We want to help others while helping ourselves.

Basically, we want what we don't have. We want more money and more time to enjoy the things money can buy.

Isn't that true for you?

Truth is, most of us aren't free to live where we choose—in a house and a neighborhood we love—because we simply can't afford it.

Today, tens of millions of people aren't living their dreams at all, are they?

THE TRUTH ABOUT THE AMERICAN DREAM

What else do we want? A top-notch education for our kids... spending time with old friends and making new friends... travel and vacations... entertainment... recreation... going out to dinner... new clothes... and a whole host of other possessions and possibilities for realizing our dreams.

13

So what happens? We finally get that special car we want—and then we stay home because we can't afford to go out! Unfortunately, we're forced to pick just one of the things we really want—and sacrifice everything else.

We've made a habit of settling for less—settling for less as a lifestyle!

Today, people aren't free to do what they'd really love to do for a living—what they're really good at. They're strapped to a job they don't like—or worse, one they hate—because they just have to have that paycheck to survive.

I've done that—working for $5.50 an hour building boats for someone making a whole lot more money than I was. Waiting on tables for $150 a week (including tips!). Doing work I hated. Hanging out with my buddies after work. Going nowhere in a hurry.

That's when I asked myself, "Is that all there is?" I used to hear that song in my sleep! "Is that all there is, my friend?"

My life was in the pits, yet I was too scared to leave and take a chance on something better. I knew I was worth more than $5.50 an hour. But I depended on that paycheck—and I had a family depending on me!

Sound familiar?

You know, the truth is less than 1% of the people in America make over $100,000 a year. And that's just about how much it takes today to even get close to financial security.

THE BOTTOM LINE

The cornerstone of the American Dream has always been financial freedom—enough money to do what you want, when you want to do it.

That's not to say that money alone is what we desire most. We all know it's not the money, but what the money will buy. As the famous restaurateur Toots Shor used to say, "I don't want to be a millionaire. I just want to live like one." And it's true that one thing money does buy in a society like ours—is freedom.

Money builds churches and schools and puts clothes on our children's backs.

Another thing money can buy today is good health.

14

The rising cost of medical care in the United States has made it virtually impossible for people of average means to afford even basic medicines and proper health care. Truth is, people can't afford to get sick anymore!

What about adequate health insurance coverage? Did you know that nearly 50 million Americans have no health insurance? It's pretty sad when almost 17% of the people under 65 years of age—in the richest country in the world—are one automobile accident or catastrophic illness away from being forced into bankruptcy!

And is there any greater cause of stress—which more and more physicians say is a primary contributor to sickness and disease—than anxiety and worry over money?

The shocking truth is that medical research proves the affluent are significantly healthier than the average American! You bet money can buy health—and lots of it!

How about happiness? They say it's the one thing money can't buy.

We all know that's not true. Just look at a child on Christmas morning.

Freedom, security, money, health, and happiness. We were never meant to be forced to pick just one or two. I say we deserve them all!

PAYING THE PRICE

Sir James Barrie, who wrote the classic fairy tale *Peter Pan*, once said:

"Dreams do come true… You can have anything in life if you will sacrifice everything else for it."

Can you believe that? Do we really have to give up everything else to get a little of what we want?

How much freedom do you have if you can't pay the mortgage or the rent?

What happiness is there if you don't have security?… if you can't afford good health and medical care? (Or if you have to work yourself to death to pay the taxes that subsidize the other guy's health insurance?)

What good is having anything if you have to give up everything else to get it?

No, the real American Dream is to have it all.

But the sad truth is the vast majority of people today don't stand a chance of getting what they want out of life. For them, the American Dream has become a fairy tale. A myth.

For an alarming number of people, the American Dream may even have become—the American Nightmare!

Chapter Two

Why?

*This is America. You
can do anything here.*
—Ted Turner
cable TV pioneer

Walt Disney once said, "All our dreams can come true—if we have the courage to pursue them."

If what Uncle Walt said is true, then the only thing standing between people and their dreams is "the courage to pursue them."

Let's talk about that for a minute.

Was it a lack of courage that made us "put away the childish things" we dreamed of as kids? Was it lack of courage that forced us to give up the dreams and aspirations of becoming a ballerina—baseball star—doctor—actor—astronaut... and settle into something more reasonable?

Was it a lack of courage that sent high school grads into four years of college—at a cost of $40,000 a year or more—only to graduate and find there weren't any jobs for them? (Or if they did find a job, it sure wasn't anything they studied in college... anything they'd spent years learning how to do... anything they really enjoyed doing).

Was it a lack of courage that got millions of blue-collar men and women laid off as "dinosaur" industries died out... as business after business closed, as farms were bought up by big corporations, and as advancing technology made tens of thousands of jobs obsolete?

Unemployed auto workers in Detroit... steel workers in Pittsburgh... coal miners in West Virginia... oil riggers in Houston, and thousands and thousands of small farmers throughout North America—do these people all simply lack courage, like Uncle Walt said?

Was it a lack of courage that makes hundreds of thousands of smart, committed, hard-working white-collar workers loyally give the best years of their lives to "The Company"—only to find their pay slashed at Northwest Airlines... their pension eliminated at United Airlines... or their "safe, secure jobs" threatened by layoffs at Dell Computer... or their "lifetime careers" bought out for a few thousand dollars at Ford, GM, and Delphi?

What about the huge layoffs that major corporations are scheduling, despite record profits in the stock market? Citicorp is outsourcing entire departments to India, even as their gross profits continue to increase. Globalization has become "gobble-ization," as American jobs are getting gobbled up by 20-cents-an-hour labor in Asia and Eastern Europe. To quote the marketing slogan for a horror flick, western workers should... "Be afraid. Be very afraid."

How about the millions of men and women struggling from paycheck to paycheck in highly competitive industries like real estate, insurance, sales, auto dealerships, hotels, food service, etc...? Did these people really all just lack the courage it takes to pursue their dreams?

Was it a lack of courage that forced more than 2 million Americans—*that's almost one of every 50 households—to file for bankruptcy?*

Was it a lack of courage that stripped tens of millions of strong, hard-working men and women of their pensions, forcing retirees to greet shoppers at Wal-Mart or work the counters at Kinkos to pay for their prescriptions?

Really—is it the lack of courage that's missing? Is that why we don't have our dreams?

WHAT ABOUT YOUR DREAMS?

Are you living and working the way you thought you would—the way you wanted—the way you would choose?

Do you have what you dreamed of as a child...?

What you went to college for...?

Were you rewarded by your company for your years of hard work and loyalty?

Will you able to retire like you want to? And after retirement, when you finally have the time… will you have the money to enjoy your life, your family, and your friends?

According to Mr. Disney, if your dreams haven't come true, it's because you didn't have the courage to pursue them.

Is that really true?

Are we really all just a bunch of cowards…?

NONSENSE!

I truly believe that each and every one of us has an inner fire, a basic survival instinct, to fight back when the chips are down.

We're not cowards—neither are our friends, our families, our children.

I guarantee you, none of us lacks courage! We don't need a pep talk—what we need is a 21st century vehicle to drive us to our dreams.

SO, WHAT'S WRONG WITH THIS PICTURE?

I'll tell you what I think—we're frustrated. Fact is, we're more than frustrated—we're angry! And we feel powerless to change the way things are.

You and I may be mad as hornets, but there sure doesn't seem to be much we can do about it—or is there?

Folks, the American Dream is not a myth. It's real—very real.

Don't you dare let anybody steal your dreams from you!

We're not cowards. We're victims of a crime! The crime of the century. Somebody stole the American Dream!

And it's not so much the American Dream itself that they took from us because we both know the dream is still there—somewhere.

What they stole was the vehicle that delivered it.

What they stole was our ability to achieve it.

What they stole was our belief that we can have it.

It's part of a cover-up that keeps telling us, "Do what everybody else is doing… Don't rock the boat … Hey, you could lose what little you've got now—don't blow it!… stay where you are, there is no other way."

19

No wonder that by age 65, nearly 95% of all Americans are either dead, dead broke, still working… or dependent upon family, church, or state. Take away Social Security, and one out of every two senior citizens in the U.S. would immediately descend into poverty. By the time we reach our "Golden Age," only 5% of Americans are financially independent! That's not only sad—it's unacceptable!

I challenge you to quit doing what 95% of the people do—which is to end up at age 65 struggling to get by on Social Security subsidized by a minimum-wage job.

In the coming pages, I'm going to show you how you can have everything you've ever dreamed of by becoming one of those special 5%-ers! So keep dreaming… and keep reading to discover how to recover your American Dream.

Who Stole The American Dream— And Why

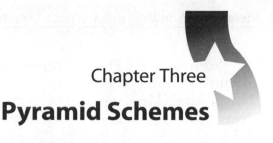

Chapter Three

Pyramid Schemes

He who wishes to be rich in a day
will be hanged in a year.
—Leonardo da Vinci
Italian artist & inventor

Y ou've probably heard some people call Network Marketing a "pyramid scheme." Do you know what that means? The reason I ask is that most people have no idea what a pyramid scheme really is.

The truth is a multi-level pyramid is a natural structure. Every single organization in the world that distributes goods and services or coordinates activities of any kind is shaped like a pyramid, with multiple levels that get bigger and wider as they go down.

Here's how noted author and educator Dr. Karl Dean Black explains it:

> "Delegation creates a multi-level pyramid. Our government is a multi-level pyramid. So are our schools and churches. All successful businesses, because they distribute goods and services, end up shaped like a multi-level pyramid. In any multi-level structure, the power comes from the bottom. Our government distributes services down a pyramid, but we give it power from the bottom with our votes. Marketing companies distribute products down a pyramid, but we give them power from the bottom with our dollars. So pyramids set up a flow that runs both ways: first down, then up. Value flows down the pyramid; power, in response, flows up. If value stops flowing down, then power (in the form of dollars or votes) stops flowing up, and the system collapses."

So, according to Dr. Black, American business, government, and education—are all pyramids.

Network Marketing is indeed a pyramid, just like Microsoft, General Motors, colleges and universities, the U.S. government, the Girl Scouts of America, franchises, and your church.

So, it's not the pyramid structure itself that makes something a "pyramid scheme." There's nothing wrong with the concept of a pyramid. It's what people do with it—how they use or abuse it that makes a pyramid good or bad, right or wrong.

TWO SIDES OF THE PYRAMID COIN

A good analogy would be cell phones.

The cell phone is just an instrument, a tool with enormous power and convenience. But cell phones are intrinsically neutral, neither good nor bad. Whether it's being used for good or bad purposes... for legal or illegal acts... is up to the operator.

For example, if someone falls in a restaurant and can't get up, and someone uses their cell phone to call 911 for help, that's a good thing.

If a different patron at the same restaurant goes outside and calls in a bomb threat to the courthouse, that's a bad thing.

It's not the cell phone itself that's good or bad. The goodness or badness depends on the actions of the operator, not the phone.

It's the same with a pyramid. There's nothing wrong with something having a pyramid structure. What makes something a pyramid "scheme" is when, as Dr. Black pointed out, "value stops flowing down..." when value is superseded by greed or illegal activities.

Now, this may surprise you, but there are two different kinds of pyramid schemes: illegal pyramid schemes... and legal pyramid schemes.

The organizational structures of both schemes are shaped like an equilateral triangle—broad at the base, pointed at the top. As you're about to learn, it's not the shape that determines whether a pyramid is an illegal scheme or a legal one. It's a matter of people and politics.

In the coming pages, we'll look at some classic illegal pyramids, as well as some powerful "legal" pyramids that are legal by law but favor the few at the top at the expense of the multitude at the bottom.

24

Chapter Four

Illegal Pyramid Schemes

*Golden Rule principles are just as
necessary for operating a business as
trucks, typewriters, and twine.*
—J.C. Penney
founder, JCPenney stores

An illegal pyramid scheme is a money-making scam wherein the people at the bottom put money in, but value doesn't flow back down to them. It's the kind of thing where a few people at the top get rich, while the majority of people—the ones on the bottom—lose out.

Examples are chain letters and the "airplane game," money-tree games that come back around every few years until the government steps in and shuts them down.

HOW A CHAIN LETTER WORKS

One day, you get a letter or email. You may or may not know the person who sent it to you. Usually the letter is filled with compelling, even inspiring, language about prosperity… and how, if you follow a few simple steps outlined in the letter, in two to four weeks, thousands to tens of thousands of dollars will appear in your mailbox as if by magic.

Something for nothing. And here's all you have to do to get it.

Somewhere in the letter is a list of names and addresses. You take the name on the top of the list, erase it, send that person the cash or money order—$1, $5, $10, $100, whatever—and you add your name to the bottom of the list. Then you make 10 to 100 copies of the letters and send them to everybody you know.

25

There's usually a sense of urgency about all of this. The letter may encourage you to send your money and mail out your copies that same day, or within 48 hours at the most. Some letters even include threats, such as, "If you break the chain, you will be punished with a plague of poverty—or someone will put peanut butter in your TiVo box."

Seriously, some chain letters I've seen tell stories of people who lost homes, businesses, even died, because they broke the chain!

And "breaking the chain" is exactly the problem—the chain letter's fatal flaw.

If everybody who received a chain letter responded by sending money to the name on top of the list—and if all those people also sent out their own copies of the letter, and so on and so on—then everybody but the people on the very last level of the pyramid would actually receive thousands of dollars in their mailbox.

But it never happens. It can't.

The people who start the chain letter, and the ones near the top who "get in early" before it gets busted, are the only ones who stand a chance of making money—and everybody else loses out.

THE ILLEGAL LOTTERIES

Any game of chance involving money is gambling, and gambling is illegal unless it's under the vigilant eyes of local, state, and federal officials.

The U.S. Postal Service has an investigation/enforcement division whose main mission in life is to catch people like chain-letter participants, put them in jail, and throw away the key. These federal agents are relentless. They carry badges, handcuffs, guns, the whole bit. And since they are "the Feds," their power extends everywhere. IRS agents are pussycats compared to these guys.

A chain letter is an illegal lottery. Outside of Tuesday night bingo at the local church or a non-profit group's fund-raising raffle, the state and federal governments are the only people who can operate a lottery legally.

Now, another variation on this get-rich-quick, money-tree scheme is the infamous "airplane game." Here's how it's played.

THE AIRPLANE GAME

A bunch of people get together and form an imaginary "airplane." The plane has passengers, a co-pilot, and a pilot. Passengers can buy a seat on the plane for $1500, $6000, or even as high as $50,000, depending on the particular game being played.

Once you become a passenger, you must go out and recruit new passengers to buy seats on the plane for the same amount of money you paid for your seat. Each time you bring on a new passenger, you move forward one seat toward the cockpit. When you bring on enough people, you become the co-pilot... and eventually the pilot.

Now, you bring your new passengers, with their cash in hand, to a meeting. That's where they turn in their money and get a seat on the plane. That's also where you get "coached" on how to bring people into the game. The co-pilot and pilot are usually excellent coaches. You'll see why soon.

So, where does the money go? To the pilot. See, when you're the pilot, all those new passengers who came to the meeting give you their money right then and there. Ten new passengers, at $1500 each, calculates to $15,000 cash. In most airplane games, it takes four to six weeks for a new passenger to move from the back of the plane to the pilot's seat.

What does a pilot do then? Flies off into the sunset to spend his money—or buys a seat on a brand-new airplane. And when you've done it twice, hey, move up to a $6000-per-seat airplane game. Simple math shows that $6000 times 10 is $60,000—or $10,000 per week (if all goes right and the plane doesn't crash)!

But in the airplane game, what goes up, must come down. With a thud!

Airplanes crash when there aren't enough new passengers—that is, when the newest passengers on the plane run out of friends and family with $1500 to spend in hopes of hitting the pilot's jackpot. What happens then? The people who became pilots early on made a quick little fortune—and the rest of the folks are out $1500 each. Why? Because money goes up the pyramid, but value in the form of a product or service doesn't come back down.

VERY FEW WINNERS, LOTS OF LOSERS

That's the second reason these money games are illegal—they rip people off.

Somebody—and eventually lots and lots of somebodies—will break the chain or fail to recruit more new people. When one person isn't able to get enough other people to send money and letters or play the game—he or she is out. You don't get your money back. That's the risk you take.

A few people at the top make a small fortune and everyone else down at the bottom of the pyramid never gets a cent.

Some of these illegal money games (like the airplane game) require thousands of dollars of cash up front in order to play. There are lots of people out there who've lost lots and lots of money when the chain broke and the plane crashed.

And one thing is true about every one of these illegal pyramid schemes—sooner or later they always crash and burn.

In fact, when the state attorney general of New York finally busted the airplane game, they discovered it had roots in organized crime. It was started by the Mafia!

PONZI SCHEMES

There's one more category of illegal pyramid. It's called a "Ponzi scheme," named after an Italian immigrant, Carlo "Charles" Ponzi.

Ponzi came to America in the early 1900s from Canada, where he spent some time in jail for passing bad checks. He ended up rather quickly in federal prison in the U.S. for smuggling illegal aliens into the country.

If Ponzi had been a botanist, history would be forced to recognize him as the man who discovered the "money tree."

Here's what he did.

Prior to the 1920s, the post offices of the world issued what were called International Reply Coupons, which could be exchanged for postage stamps throughout the world. Ponzi's idea was to purchase these coupons in countries where the inflation rate was high and redeem them in countries where the rate was low. Simply put, this enabled him to buy low and sell high.

28

On the strength of these coupons, Ponzi created the Securities Exchange Company and issued his own "promissory notes." An investor could purchase one of Ponzi's notes with a face value of, say, $150 for only $100. In just 90 days, the investor could redeem the note for its full value. In the days when banks were regulated to offer 4% interest, Ponzi's notes promised an extraordinary return of 50%!

At first, Ponzi's investors were cautious and risked only $10 or $20. However, after earning 50% interest on their money a couple of times, they felt more secure and soon began to invest thousands. Ponzi also cut the time frame in half to only 45 days to sweeten the deal for investors. (It did!)

In no time at all, Ponzi's empire grew to staggering proportions. One million bucks would flow into his offices every day (the equivalent of $100 million in today's dollars)! As his investors got rich and spread the word, Ponzi got even richer. He was hailed as a financial genius. He now owned a local bank—the Hanover Trust Company—lived in the posh suburb of Lexington, Massachusetts, and was known far and wide as "The Great Ponzi."

MONEY MACHINE CRASHES

Only one problem.

Ponzi's "money machine" operated by robbing Peter to pay Paul. He took the money investors sent in today to pay the money due tomorrow on previous investors' notes. It was a merry-go-round of money that worked as long as the "Wizard of Ponzi" kept cranking the wheels and nobody looked behind the curtain.

And then, one day in 1920, the merry-go-round stopped dead.

Investigators discovered that the International Reply Coupons that were supposed to be the source of Ponzi's wealth-building investments didn't exist. Ponzi never purchased more than $100 worth of them, total.

A public relations man whom Ponzi had hired to handle the attacks from the Boston press took one look at what was actually going on—and blew the whistle.

Ponzi was convicted of mail fraud and sentenced to nine years in prison. He jumped bail, moved to Florida, sold swamp land in a real estate scam, got caught, and was returned again to prison. Eventually, he was deported back to Italy. Ponzi died broke and alone in 1941.

ROUND AND ROUND AND ROUND

The full amount of money lost in the Ponzi scheme will never be known. Over $15 million (in 1920 dollars) was paid out to "investors" before the "business" collapsed. Carlo "Charles" Ponzi was the proud father of one of the most incredible inventions of all time—the illegal pyramid scheme.

What made Ponzi's scam an illegal pyramid scheme was the merry-go-round principle. As long as money was coming in from new "investors," money could continue to go out to the early investors. For a time, investors were paid in full, on time, and everyone was happy.

However, when the money stopped coming in, "the jig was up" because there was no money or items of value, like stocks or CDs or real estate or gold bars held in reserve. Because Ponzi used new investors' money to line his pockets and pay off the early investors, when the flow of new money stopped, the scheme collapsed like a house of cards.

Eventually, the people who invested late in the game lost their money.

Some of them lost everything they had.

What Ponzi did was to live on the "float"—you know, like writing a check today to pay yesterday's bills based on money that won't arrive until tomorrow in the hope that the check won't be cashed until sometime next week—and so on and so on.

Sound familiar? Likely too familiar.

You know, it seems to me that a whole big part of the world of government, education, and business today is doing just what Carlo Ponzi did.

In the next chapter we'll look at several big, BIG pyramids that make Ponzi's scheme look like penny-ante poker.

To make matters worse, they're perfectly legal.

Should they continue to be legal? Or ruled illegal?

You be the judge.

Chapter Five

Legal Pyramid Schemes

Giving money and power to the U.S.
government is like giving whiskey
and car keys to a teen-age boy.
—P.J. O'Rourke
political commentator

I t should be obvious to you now why illegal pyramid schemes are, well, illegal. Illegal gambling, illegal airplane games, Ponzi schemes, and outright rip-offs that permit a select few to get rich at the expense of many others—these acts break human laws.

But there's another set of laws that govern how humans live and work. Natural laws. God's laws. It's these laws that Dr. Black was speaking about when he said that pyramids collapse when there's no value flowing down to balance the power of the dollars (or votes) flowing up.

THE BIGGEST PYRAMID SCHEME IN THE WORLD

The alarming truth is that there are many organizations and enterprises in the world that are without a doubt pyramid schemes of the highest (or more accurately, lowest) order. In fact, the biggest pyramid scheme in the entire world is legal!

The pyramid I'm talking about is run by the United States government.

It's called Social Security.

There's not a person in America under age 50 who should expect to collect all of their Social Security benefits at retirement. Everybody knows the Social Security Administration will be broke by the time all the Baby Boomers start collecting their fair share.

Really, *what is Social Security but a huge pyramid scheme?*

Here's why I say that: You pay a percentage of your earnings every month of your working life via a "payroll tax"—and a pretty big chunk it is, too—so that one day, when you retire—at what, 62... 63... 64... 65 if you live that long?—you'll get a monthly benefit check 'til the day you die.

How much do you pay in? Right now the law requires employees to pay 7.65% of their gross income up to $90,000 for Social Security and Medicare (6.2% for SS; 1.45% for Medicare). If you're self-employed, you have to pay twice—once as the employer and a second time as the employee, doubling your payroll taxes to 15.3%. Ouch, ouch!

Considering the U.S. has nearly 150 million people paying into Social Security each paycheck, that's a big chunk of change going into the Social Security Trust Fund each month.

Did I just say, "trust fund"? Double goof—there's no trust... much less a fund. Politicians call it a fund, but it's really a "funny fund" because no fund actually exists. No fund. No savings account. No CDs. No nothin' but dusty IOUs from the U.S. government.

THE REVOLVING REVENUE DOOR

So, what happens to the money that the government *takes in* from Social Security and Medicare taxes? It goes right *back out* to people eligible to draw Social Security—retirees, survivors, and the disable. What's left over goes into the general budget, and our elected officials spend it on roads (if we're lucky) or failed government programs, like the $20 billion anti-drug media campaign that the government reluctantly admits has had zero effect on illegal drug use.

In other words, when the U.S. government *uses new investor money to pay early investors and then squanders the rest, IT'S A LEGAL PYRAMID. But when Carlo Ponzi did the same thing, IT WAS AN ILLEGAL PYRAMID!*

Now, here's the really scary part. When Social Security was first enacted in 1935, there were 35 workers for every eligible person and life expectancy was around 60. In 2026, the year the government will be paying out more in Social Security benefits than it takes in with payroll taxes, there will be 2 workers for every eligible recipient—and life expectancy will be near 80.

32

So what are politicians doing to avert this looming crisis? Nothing constructive—just spouting slogans and pointing fingers at whichever party is in power.

Cue Nero's fiddle while Rome burns.

UNDER 40? CONGRATULATIONS—YOU GET TO PICK UP THE CHECK!

Right now the government is doing okay with their version of the Ponzi scheme because between 1946 and the mid-1960s, 76 million kids were born into a huge mega-group of humanity called the Baby Boom. All these millions of Boomers have been donating money into the fund all their working lives, and they're paying for those folks who are old enough to qualify for Social Security benefits right now.

But what happens when it comes time for the first of those 76 million Baby Boomers to start collecting—which will occur starting in 2008?

You guessed it... there won't be enough money to pay all those it's-my-time-to-collect Boomers! You see, after the Baby Boom came the baby bust. There have been nowhere near the same number of births since the Baby Boom—and probably never will be again. So, there will be far fewer people paying in money than there are taking it out.

In business terms that's called a negative cash flow—too much month at the end of the money!

Did you know that males who turned 30 in 1990 will pay $200,000 *more* into Social Security than they will ever take out? Fact is, 70% of American families pay more in FICA—Social Security and Medicare—than they pay in income taxes! Talk about a scam and a scheme!

What's going to happen when the first wave of baby boomers takes out so much money that there's nothing left? Your kids and grandkids will be working overtime to pay a whole bunch of old geezers to fish and play golf. If you thought there was a generation gap in the '60s, just wait until Gen X-ers start paying a thousand bucks a month (or more) in Social Security taxes so that the Boomers can live the life of Riley in Sun City, Florida.

The crash of an airplane game will be like a fly going down the toilet compared to the nationwide devastation when Social Security crashes!

33

You tell me: Is value flowing down this pyramid? Sure—in dribs and drabs until it dries up.

Sounds a lot like Carlo Ponzi's scam, doesn't it?

IT PAYS (AND PAYS... AND PAYS... AND PAYS...) TO BE AT THE TOP

The essence of all pyramid schemes—the illegal ones and the legal ones—is that the guys at the top get rich while everybody else at the bottom loses out.

It's like when corporate CEOs get paid millions and millions in pay, perks, and benefits... while the stock price takes a nosedive. Larry Ellison, the CEO of Oracle Software, for example, hauled in nearly $800 MILLION during the dot.com bust—while the company stock dropped 61%!

So, what did Ellison do while thousands of loyal Oracle employees received pink slips and tens of thousands of stockholders lost their shirts? Why, he bought the world's largest privately owned boat, a 550-foot mega-yacht costing $125 million.

The money that the guys sitting on top of the corporate pyramids make these days is nothing short of criminal—unless, of course, it *is* criminal, like Andrew Fastow of Enron and Bernie Ebbers of WorldCom, just two of the dozens of top execs who were caught with their hand in the cookie jar in the go-go years before the dot.com bubble burst. Both men were sentenced to prison for their contributions to two of the biggest corporate frauds in American history. Their greed drove their respective companies into bankruptcy, costing tens of thousands of employees their jobs and wiping out employee pensions, some of which were worth millions.

Fastow cried at his sentencing. (I, on the other hand, didn't shed so much as a tear for either of these post-Ponzi crooks).

HAVE YOU NO SHAME?

Meanwhile, the rest of the top dogs at public companies are taking payouts just as big as Fastow and Ebbers, but, eager to stay out of prison, cautious CEOs are stuffing their pockets with perfectly legal tactics—oversized paychecks and an obscene number of stock options.

Since 1980, average CEO pay has skyrocketed 442%, while average worker pay has inched up less than 2% during the same time period. How piggish is CEO pay? The average CEO of a Fortune 100 company makes nearly $15 MILLION PER YEAR. Compare that to the average worker, who makes less than $30,000 per year. If average worker pay had grown at the same rate of CEO pay since 1980, workers would be earning $164,000 a year instead of $30,000.

You know CEO pay is out of control when pro-business *Fortune* magazine featured a smiling pig in a suit on their cover with this headline: *CEO Pay: Have They No Shame?*

American CEOs are the worst abusers. CEOs in the U.S. are paid more than twice as much as Canadian CEOs... three times more than British CEOs... and four times more than German CEOs.

Have you no shame, indeed?

IT'S GOOD TO BE CEO

Fact is, if you're a CEO, it even pays to fail.

Michael Eisner, former head of Disney, is the poster boy for CEOs who are overpaid for being under-producers. During the 10 years Eisner headed up Disney, the stock gained 1.9%, compared to the 9.1% average return for the Fortune 500 companies.

So, what did Eisner earn for his dismal performance? A total of $950 million, which calculates to nearly *$2 million A WEEK* for each of his 500 weeks at the helm.

If that's not enough, top executives are routinely given stock options worth tens of millions as part of their compensation package. Problem with stock options is that Congress passed a law saying companies don't have to expense the options it gives to top managers. Which means giant, multi-national companies can give away hundreds of millions of shares worth hundreds of billions of dollars and not have to report it to the SEC or stockholders, who are the ones subsidizing the giveaways.

Last time I looked, there were more than 30 CEOs of Fortune 500 companies who are in line to receive more than $100 MILLION EACH in stock options. And that's on top of their multi-million-dollar annual paychecks! One CEO, William W. McGuire of UnitedHealth

Group, is sitting on—now get this—MORE THAN $1.6 BILLION in company stock.

Pretty good deal if you're a big honcho in a corner office, huh? What's the damage to the little people at the bottom of the pyramid? Billions of dollars OUT of stockholders' pockets and INTO top-of-the-pyramid execs' pockets—and it's all perfectly legal.

By the way—do you know who determines the CEO's pay at these major corporations? The board of directors. And guess who has the biggest say when it comes to choosing members of the board? You've got that right—the CEO himself!

But, hey, that's business—it's not personal.

Right—you mean, like the business of government?

PAYING FOR PERFORMANCE

Tell me, does it make sense to you to raise the pay of congressmen and senators who've been running "U.S.A., Inc." at a loss—not billions, but trillions, of dollars!—for generations?

And then our "elected leaders" have the nerve to set up a cushy pension plan that will pad their pockets for years after they're voted out of office—even if they only serve one term! No wonder politicians have a bad name!

Look, you're a "stockholder" in this country. We all are. How do you feel about the performance of the executives and managers in your government? Remember, these guys work for us! And remember, too, these are the people who provide the military with $650 hammers and $6,000 toilets!

Not their money, not their problem.

Does all this make sense to you?

We pour in money (politicians call it "revenues;" we citizens call it "taxes"), and the politicians spend us into the poor house, despite record revenues flowing into the IRS (why not?... they aren't accountable until the next election, right?). As one political observer put it, *"... in recent years, Washington, wrestling with the budget deficit, has come to resemble more and more a drunk wrestling with alcoholism."*

How does the U.S. compare to other countries? Well, thanks to huge deficits and a looming Social Security and Medicare crisis that our politicians refuse to act on, the World Economic Forum ranked the U.S. sixth in global competitiveness, behind Nigeria, Peru, Uganda, Venezuela, and Vietnam!

CORPORATE WELFARE—A NATIONAL SHAME

What about government-supported "corporate welfare"? How's that for money going up the pyramid and no value coming down? Talk about fleecing the American public! Federal corporate welfare programs cost American taxpayers *$150 billion annually*—while the federal deficit spins out of control!

Everybody applauded when Congress passed "workfare" laws that reduced welfare roles by as much as 50%. However, corporate "wealthfare" in the form of tax breaks, subsidies, and grants to huge corporations has risen to *$150 billion a year*, which, if rescinded, would reduce our federal deficit by 50% within one year!

Not surprisingly, the biggest hogs feeding at the tax-funded trough are also the biggest political contributors (surprise, surprise!). Archer Daniels Midland (ADM), the world's biggest agricultural processor and distributor, has received more than $3 billion since the mid-'90s in subsidies for ethanol; meanwhile, ethanol prices have spiked through the roof and, as a result, ADM is earning record profits.

Meanwhile, the corporate wealthfare tax breaks to ADM continue.

Haven't heard enough? Here's another corporate wealthfare boondoggle: Since 1999, Wal-Mart, the world's biggest and most profitable company, has received *more than a billion dollars* in subsidies, tax breaks, free land, and cash grants to build stores and distribution centers in 240 locations across 35 states.

It's scandalous that a multi-national company with $10 billion in annual profits receives a dime of taxpayer money, much less billions of dollars in benefits. Why is the U.S. government playing Robin Hood in reverse, shaking down the poor and middle class, in order to hand out $100-plus-billion a year to Fortune 500 companies that are raking in record profits?

Employing lobbyists as the middlemen, corporations are slicing a large piece of the their profit pie and depositing it into politicians' pocketbooks. Come to think of it, maybe the American Dream isn't being stolen after all.

It's being sold to the highest bidder.

Corporate welfare is armed robbery using politicians instead of a pistol! Even Ponzi himself couldn't have thought of scams as outrageous as these!

PAYING YOUR UNFAIR SHARE OF TAXES

Do you think it's fair that individuals, many of whom struggle from paycheck to paycheck, are paying more in income taxes while humongous corporations earning billions each year are paying less?

Fair? No. Fact? Yes.

In the 1950s, 28% of federal revenues came from corporate taxes. Today, corporate revenues represent only 7% of all federal tax receipts, a 75% DECREASE.

Who picks up the difference? Individual taxpayers, that's who. You and me, that's who. Meanwhile, the corporate fat cats exchange high five's and award themselves more stock options.

Could it be the U.S. government is a legal pyramid scheme? I hate to think so, but look at the facts: Our "leaders" in Washington have run up a $5 TRILLION national debt while penning laws with loopholes that enable major corporations to pay less and less taxes. Meanwhile, Congress authorizes the IRS to pay outside agencies 24% commission to collect back taxes from individual taxpayers.

Let's see—the IRS is terrorizing the little people while sipping martinis with the corporate fat cats. Is this what the founding fathers had in mind when forming a new nation? Don't think so.

As for the IRS, it's choking on incompetence and bureaucratic red tape. The IRS recently spent $8 billion of our tax dollars to overhaul its computer programs. What we got for that money was, a top official admitted, "a system that does not work in the real world."

Here's proof. The IRS sends out 30 million tax penalty notices each year. *Yet, according to their own admission, nearly 50% are incorrect!* This is an agency that is so incompetent that they couldn't account for 64% of their budget at a year-end audit.

The IRS is worse than a pyramid scheme. At least Ponzi knew how much money he was stealing!

WHAT ABOUT THE 'REAL' AMERICAN DREAM?

Winning the lottery… we still have that, right?

Sure we do. Hey, new millionaires are created every month in 40 (and growing) weekly state lotteries around the country. It's legalized gambling, generating more revenue than casinos, and the government is in on it! Americans spend $45 billion per year on state lotteries. Half of all Americans play the lottery at least occasionally, spending an average of $155 a year on tickets, more than they spend on books and movies combined.

Just look at the lines of people buying lottery tickets—who's playing? The people who can least afford to play, right? This is crazy! You've got a better chance of being hit by lightning—twice—than winning the lottery!

So who's really the winner? The government bureaucrats and administrators—once again, the fat cats at the top. Everybody else loses. Wait a minute… isn't that the definition of an illegal pyramid scheme? Aren't they playing a money merry-go-round, just like Ponzi did?

Nah, it's legal because the government's running it—and besides, all that money is supposed to go for new roads and bridges and public schools and….

Yeah, right!

Where's the money really going? In what direction is the value really flowing? Not down to you and me, that's for sure.

Oh, I almost forgot about two of our favorite sacred cows….

CHARITY AND EDUCATION

Charities like the United Way are do-good, non-profit organizations that we can trust, right? Wrong. Non-profit for you and me, maybe… but all too often, BIG profits for the hypocrites who run them!

A former director of the United Way was paid $463,000 a year plus perks—including 10 free trips a year to Las Vegas for "business" (yeah, monkey business). Get this: Thirty-three different non-profit organizations, including the Boy Scouts of America, pay their directors over $200,000 a year!

In many non-profits, less than 5% of the revenues is actually spent helping the victims, while 95% goes to pay expenses, including—you guessed it—the salaries, expense accounts, medical benefits, and retirement packages for administrators and directors. And you thought all your money went to kids and cancer research.

Not!

What about a college education?—oh, there's a great one! They call it "higher education" because that's where the costs are headed every year—higher!

Tell me, where else can you spend $40,000, $50,000, or $60,000 a year for four years (or more) to receive a piece of paper that doesn't even guarantee you a decent job?

Who gets the good jobs right out of college? With the exception of the top jocks who turn to pro sports, it's those very, very few at the top of their class in those few top universities—the ones that cost a fortune. Sounds a tad exclusive—kind of like the airplane game?

For the last 20 years, college costs have tripled, increasing at about twice the rate of inflation. As I write this, the average loan debt for students with loans is $19,000. According to *USA Today*, parents in their 20s "...will need to save nearly $5,000 a year for 18 years to put one child through college."

Scary to think, but college tuition is rising faster than medical care in this country. And where does the lion's share of this burgeoning tuition go? Mostly to the faculty and staff, of course.

Nearly two-thirds of tuition goes to paying salaries of employees. Full-tenured professors earn an average of $80,000 a year, plus free health insurance and fat retirement pensions. Add to that the extra income many professors receive from textbook sales... book store sales... consulting fees... royalties on patented products... and speaking fees—it's not uncommon for professors to earn $2... $3... $5... even $10 million dollars a year from sideline enterprises WITHOUT TEACHING A SINGLE CLASS (their unpaid grad students do most of the teaching).

I tell you, it's a legal pyramid scheme!

More and more dollars are flowing up the higher-ed pyramid, but less and less value is flowing down. A college degree used to guarantee you a good job with a growing company. Now all it guarantees is the night shift at the local Starbucks.

ILLUSION VS. REALITY

Most people are under the illusion that they'll graduate from college and walk right into a solid career opportunity. Boy, are they ever in for a reality check! That kind of thinking reminds me of the story about a man who died and went to Purgatory.

The archangel in charge explained to the man that he could choose between going to Heaven or Hell, but once he made the choice—that was it. The man asked if he could see them both before he made his final choice. The archangel said, "Sure."

When they got to Heaven, it was beautiful. Everybody was smiling. It was peaceful and tranquil—just perfect. The people seemed content and so happy. It certainly looked very lovely indeed.

"This is beautiful," the man said. "May I see the other now?" The archangel took him down to Hell.

It was incredible—one huge party! People were laughing and dancing, the music was blaring. There was a lavish spread of magnificent food, everybody was drinking and carrying on. The man had never seen anything like it in his life, and his eyes grew as big as silver dollars.

The archangel leaned over to him and asked, "Well, which do you choose?"

"Oh, this one—this one!" said the man excitedly. "I want to be in Hell."

The archangel reminded the man that he only had one choice. "Are you certain you want to be in Hell?" The archangel asked the man. "Oh, yes—I'm positive," came the reply.

The archangel clapped his hands and, in a flash, the music stopped, the party disappeared, and the man found himself chained to a post with flames shooting at him from every direction.

"No!" he cried to another suffering soul. "Where did the party go—the people, the dancing, all the food?"

"Oh," said the suffering soul, "you must have attended the marketing presentation. This is what Hell is really like."

THE AGE OF THE PROFESSIONAL STUDENT

The moral of the story? Things are not always what they appear to be—

just ask the college graduates who have to move back home because they can't find a job in their field!

Today, moving back home after college is the rule, not the exception. That's why they're being called the "Boomerang Generation"—they get tossed out, only to come spinning back home again. What college is best at preparing people for is—more college. Get a degree, then another, and another.

"Do what I do and you, too, can become a professional student."

In 1960, we graduated 9,733 Ph.D.s. Today, more than 40,000 students earn a Ph.D. each year! Where do they all go? Back to college to teach others how to get a Ph.D. so that they can go back to college to teach others how to get a Ph.D.

Do you see a pattern here?

Folks, it's time we all took a reality check. Let's face it, when you try to use your B.S. degree to achieve job security and financial independence, you'll find out what "BS" really stands for—"Back to School"—because that's where you'll head when you can't find a job.

ADD UP THE DREAM DEBT

Are you beginning to see how legal pyramid schemes are robbing you of your opportunity to achieve the American Dream?

Just look at the list of dream stealers again—a soon-to-be-bankrupt Social Security system… outsized CEO pay and unaccounted for stock options… corporate "wealthfare" that decreases corporate taxes while increasing your personal taxes… trillions of dollars in national debt supported by loans from decades-long enemies like Russia and China… college tuition costs increasing at twice the rate of inflation… and an IRS that goes after individual taxpayers while playing footsie with corporate cash cows.

You get the feeling the deck is being stacked against you? It reminds me of the old poker saying: If you sit down at a poker table, look around to see who the sucker is, and if you can't spot one, then get up and leave 'cause the sucker is YOU!

I don't like being played for a sucker, especially when it comes to my dreams.

How about you?

Chapter Six

There Is No Security Anymore

*Too many people are thinking of security
instead of opportunity; they seem to be
more afraid of life, than of death.*
—James F. Byrnes
Sec. of State under Pres. Truman

Why a chapter on security?
Because security is what people want most in their lives. All the research shows that security continues to top the list of what people desire in their careers, for their families, and for their futures, too.

The unhappy truth is that today, security is slipping away—or is gone—for most of us. And it's going at an alarming rate.

But security is the cornerstone of the American Dream—isn't it? We want secure manufacturing jobs. We want secure white-collar jobs. We want secure government jobs.

That's what people want. Problem is there's no more security in the old, antiquated way of doing business.

Just ask the millions upon millions of employees who have been laid off from secure jobs with "blue chip" companies during the past decade. Even in the face of the most massive layoffs since the Great Depression, people still think they can find security by working for a traditional business.

It reminds me of a story.

'I'M STICKING TO MY STORY'

One night a guy decided to drop by a local bar after work to have a drink with his friends. Everybody was having a great time! Swapping stories... singing along with the juke box... buying rounds of drinks for the table.

Before he knew it, he and his friends had closed the place down. As he stumbled to his car, he could see the sun breaking over the horizon. He glanced at his watch. 6 a.m. "Oh, no," he thought to himself. "I've done it again. My wife will kill me... I promised her no more all-night binges!"

Twenty minutes later he pulled into the driveway, rehearsing the excuse he thought up on the way home. As he stumbled through the front door, he looked up to see his wife waiting for him with her arms crossed.

"Where have you been all night?" she demanded. He straightened up, looked her right in the eye, and slurred, "I got home just after midnight, and I didn't want to wake you... so I slept in the hammock outside."

His wife glared at him and responded. "Nice try... only one problem... we took the hammock down two years ago!"

The man gave her a startled look and then blurted, *"Well, that's my story and I'm sticking to it!"*

My friend, people who think they can have the same job security today that workers enjoyed in the 1950s are just kidding themselves... they're telling themselves a ridiculous lie... and then sticking to it.

In the words of workplace consultant Mary Lynn Pulley:

> "The rules that people grew up with about lifetime security and employment no longer work."

Let's face it, there is no security anymore. We can't turn back the clock. It's time to tell yourself the truth, prepare yourself for the consequences—and get on with your life!

A BRAVE NEW WORLD

Today, it takes at least two incomes for most Americans to achieve the standard of living our parents had with one paycheck. And even that's

44

a stretch: People are now talking about the three-income family as if that were normal!

Things are changing so fast in our world and workplace that people who had iron-clad, lifelong positions with solid companies just a few short years ago are out of work today.

Did you know that 30% of all Americans lost their jobs during the last two decades of the 20th century?—that's 3 out of every 10 workers! And as globalization... outsourcing... and automation continue at a galloping pace, that trend will continue for decades to come.

Blue-collar workers were the first to go, replaced by automation and advanced technology, as entire industries were transformed, seemingly overnight. White-collar workers were the next to feel the ax, as sophisticated computer systems replaced whole departments of clerical workers.

Telephone operators are a perfect example. In the days before powerful personal computers, "Ma Bell" and her rivals employed several hundred thousand operators to handle local and long distance calls.

Today, one high-tech AT&T supervisor monitoring a souped-up software system can do the work it used to take 10,000 live operators to do—and automation will do it better, faster, and cheaper.

I'm no big fan of voice mail, but voice recognition software has become so good that entire industries as laying off receptionists and service reps. Today, it's nearly impossible to get a "live" person on the phone when you call your credit card company... mortgage company... bank... or insurance company.

Where do all those laid off workers go for employment after they're kicked to the curb by automation? Starbucks or The Home Depot, if they're lucky. Wal-Mart, if they're not.

And it's gonna get worse, trust me.

Since 2001, there has been only one private sector in the U.S. economy that has added jobs—health care. In the five years since the dot.com bubble burst, health care has added 1.7 million jobs. The rest of the private sector? Zero.

As the Boomers age, health care will continue to add jobs. Millions of them, in fact. So, if you want to escort senior citizens to dinner at the local assisted living facility... change sheets and empty bed pans at a nursing home, then you're in the right place at the right time.

Here's what *Fortune* magazine says about today's "new" economy:

"American factories are lean (with 12% fewer employees than at the 1979 peak), strong (producing 51% more stuff), and fast (increasing productivity at a torrid 3.5% annual rate)."

That's why economist Paul Pilzer's prediction of 20% unemployment in major industrialized nations early in the 21st century isn't far-fetched—manufacturing efficiencies are cutting workers right out of the loop! Personally, I don't predict 20% UNEMPLOYMENT. There will always be entry-level jobs available at McDonald's and the night shift at Circle K convenience stores. I am, however, predicting 20% to 80% UNDER-EMPLOYMENT, as millions will be forced to take low-skilled, low-paying jobs they're over qualified for.

Not a pretty picture, is it?

A BRIEF HISTORY LESSON IN CHANGE

Most of us can accept that certain industries are born, grow, prosper, get old, and eventually die. That's just the way it is. And it's foolish to hang on to the past and fight progress.

Around the turn of the 20th century, we were a land of farmers. Nearly 90% of the population was involved in producing the food we needed as a nation. In 1930 there were 30 million farmers in the U.S., and they fed about 100 million citizens.

Fast-forward 70 years to the year 2000.

Guess how many farmers were working the land as we entered the new millennium: Amazingly, fewer than 300,000 farmers are needed to feed 300 million Americans, plus another 100 million people throughout the rest of the world. In only 70 years, just 1% of the farmers are producing four times as much food! Incredible!

So what has happened to all those displaced farmers and their children? The sons and daughters of farmers today are business owners, software programmers, chemical engineers, insurance salesmen, doctors, and lawyers—not farmers. Why should they be? There's no security in farming anymore—and, unless you inherited thousands of acres, there's little opportunity left in farming.

CUT... OR BE CUT

Steel workers, auto workers, machinists, seamstresses—the jobs that our economy depended upon just a few short decades ago—are disappearing fast. To stay competitive today, businesses must increase production and lower costs. And that means more machines and fewer people.

Let's get real here—industries that hang on to workers they don't really need may be looked upon as kinder and gentler, but not when they're forced out of business and into bankruptcy because they can't compete.

It just doesn't make sense to continue to pay three full-time workers $30,000 a year each if they can be replaced by a machine that costs $50,000—a machine that never makes mistakes... never takes a vacation... doesn't go on strike for higher wages... doesn't require a benefit package with a pension... and will never file a sexual harassment lawsuit.

About the only secure job left in this country is a Supreme Court judge 'cause they're appointed for life! Only trouble is, there are only nine of them, and most of them look to be in pretty good health.

Take my advice—don't wait by the phone.

GET AN EDUCATION

Going to college, getting a good job, providing a secure future for yourself and your family isn't what it used to be. It's a myth, isn't it?

Sure, they teach you a lot in college. But none of the professors teach you how to become financially secure. It reminds me of a poem by Stephen Crane, the author of *The Red Badge of Courage*:

I met a seer.
He held in his hands
The book of wisdom.
"Sir," I addressed him,
"Let me read."

"Child—" he began.
"Sir," I said, "Think not that I am a child,
For already I know much
Of that which you hold.
Aye much."
He smiled.
Then he opened the book
And held it before me—
Strange that I should have
Grown so suddenly blind.

The "book of wisdom" that tells you how to achieve the American Dream doesn't exist in any college library. Even if it did, only a very few college students would be able to understand a word of it.

The job market for college grads is bad and getting worse! Why? Demographics, plain and simple. The Baby Boom that created the most awesome market for goods and services the world has ever seen... that created the most massive block of college graduates... also created the most cut-throat, competitive job market ever!

That's why the clerk at the local Starbucks and the checkout girl at the local Borders book store are college grads—they've got a diploma, but unfortunately, all the good jobs are already filled by people with diplomas *and experience*. Sorry, Mr. and Ms. Generation X, we're not hiring.

The night shift at the nursing home down the street is hiring, though....

GET A JOB

We've lost as many as a quarter of a million jobs in a single month—and that figure is destined to get higher and higher—and that doesn't include the millions of people whose jobless benefits have run out and who've given up and quit looking for work!

Are there jobs out there? Sure—lots of 'em. The classified ad section in the local newspaper is as thick as the yellow pages. But 90% of those jobs can be summed up in two hyphenated words: dead-end, low-paying.

Thanks, but no thanks.

The number of men and women changing jobs every year now is astonishing! It used to be that you'd get into an industry and there you'd stay 'til you retired. Maybe you'd make one or two changes to move up the corporate ladder. But today, employment experts expect people to have 10 to 12 different jobs in five to six different careers during their working lives! Where's the security in that?

I tell you, there is no security anymore.

Even the most secure job in the world, working for the U.S. Postal Service, is in jeopardy these days. Currently, the postal service employs more than 700,000 people. But with the advent of e-mail and increasing competition from UPS and FedEx, the postal service has automated scores of back-office functions, resulting in the Postal Service's goal of eliminating 13,000 jobs a year for the next 10 years.

NON-TRADITIONAL LABOR ON THE INCREASE

No matter where you turn—with very, very few exceptions—there simply is no more security in the American workplace today. That's why nearly 35 million Americans—close to one-third of the work force— are contingency workers, including independent contractors, part-time employees, consultants, freelancers, the self-employed, and contract labor.

What this tells me is that free enterprise is no longer free. Most people don't have that most American of all rights, a choice. They have to take what they can get.

There's no freedom in that—and no security, either.

THE WONDERFUL WORLD OF OWNING A CONVENTIONAL SMALL BUSINESS

Remember what I said in the Introduction—more than 90% of all conventional small businesses fail within the first five years. Of the 10% that survive, very few will ever see year 10. How many 10-year-old, non-franchised businesses do you know of?

The truth is that most small business entrepreneurs don't own their own businesses—they own their own jobs!

I know from firsthand experience.

49

I had my own business when I was 24 years old. I got fed up working for someone else and decided to strike out on my own. Unfortunately, I quickly found out that I was like the lawyer who has himself for a client—*I was working for a crazy person*!

I put in one frantic year of 80-plus-hour weeks. The good news is that all my hard work paid off. I made a million dollars my first full year in my new cellular phone business. The bad news is it cost me $1.2 million to earn it! Talk about an expensive education!

I can hear you now, "Maybe you should have gone to college, Burke." Well, I did that, too. I've got a college degree in criminal justice to prove it. Hey, you wouldn't happen to have a job for a prison warden in training, would you? Trust me, working as a cop or a probation officer is not the best vehicle for becoming financially independent!

FRANCHISING

Many people today turn to franchising as an alternative to starting their own high-risk business from scratch.

To get into the franchise business, you pay money in the form of a licensing fee to a franchisor, who hands you what's called a "turn-key" business operation. Everything is already researched, developed, designed, and set up for you—from advertising to the proper equipment to use. You learn how to train your people, do your books, make your products, get your supplies, and so on. You just pay your money, turn the key, and drive off into the sunset of success, right?

Wrong.

You see, there's one major problem—when you add up the costs of leasing your space, remodeling it, buying the equipment, paying for inventory, etc... the average franchise costs $100,000-plus just to open the doors!

What's more, you've got a 7-day week of 12- to 14-hour days managing a bunch of minimum-wage employees. And, if you're very good, after three to five years, you'll break even and be able to start making a profit.

Most owner-operated franchises today provide about a $50,000 to $60,000 annual income for the owner once the initial investment is all paid off—if the owner works as the manager. Hire a manager, and you're lucky to break even.

You can earn more if you can afford one of the bigger and better franchises. McDonald's franchises are virtually fail-safe. But you'll pay a steep price for your profits. A McDonald's franchise costs more than $1 million to get off the ground!

According to Jane Bryant Quinn, business columnist for *Newsweek*, one-third of all franchisees loses money... one-third breaks even... and one-third makes a profit.

That means 66 out of every 100 franchisees fail to make a profit! Hey, that's better odds than playing the lottery, but that's little consolation if you're one of the two out of three franchisees who have to shut the doors or sell your business for a loss!

Experienced, professional franchisees today will tell you that unless you're going to own a string of five or more successful stores—it's just not worth the hassle.

Help!

The simple fact is we can't depend on help from the outside.

Somebody once said that "Hope is the expectation that something or somebody is going to come along and save you." Sorry, but Cinderella has already claimed that fairy tale. The reality is there is no hope for most people with conventional jobs in conventional industries. The institutions of education, government, and business can no longer be counted on to provide us with the opportunity to accomplish our dreams.

We have to take matters into our own hands. And what that means in the simplest of terms is—if it's meant to be, it's up to me.

For things to change—you have to change. For things to get better—you have to get better.

So, what are you going to do?

What can you do?

Let's start by taking a look at your options.

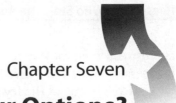

Chapter Seven

What Are Your Options?

The world is all gates, all
opportunities, strings of
tension waiting to be struck.
—Ralph Waldo Emerson
American philosopher

O kay, let's say that you accept the fact that there's no security in the work world anymore... and that "If it's going to be—it's up to me."

Where do you go?

What do you do?

Let's take a look at your income options.

YOUR INCOME OPTIONS

Option 1: A Job: That's the trading-time-for-money trap we talked about before. No matter what you earn, there's neither security nor freedom in having a job. Having a job means you are two words away from the street—"You're fired!"

Zig Ziglar, one of America's top sales motivators, once described the word JOB as "Just Over Broke." And in today's changing work world, the only for-sure-secure jobs are the few and far between ones at the very top—or the millions of menial jobs at the very bottom.

Option 2: Self-Employment: Most people fed up with being fired will turn to self employment in an effort to create more security in their work. However, as I pointed out earlier, the odds are stacked against you even for starting up the most modest of conventional small businesses—much less keeping it open and making it profitable.

If you're one of the few who make it past the first couple of years, you've got a chance, but be realistic—you have less than a 1% chance of making your business last 10 years or longer.

Option 3: Buy a Franchise: If you have a couple hundred thousand dollars to gamble (or a couple million, for that matter) you can shift the self-employment odds in your favor by buying a franchise. But with only 33% of franchises showing a profit, do you really want to risk your life savings… or mortgage your home… or borrow from your parents and put them at risk… with only a 1 in 3 chance of succeeding? You can get better odds than that at a craps table in Las Vegas….

Option 4: Investments: This is how the rich get rich and how Palm Beach socialites maintain their estates and pay their country club dues. Problem is, it takes a TON of cash to maintain even a modest retirement. A million dollars ain't what it used to be. Do the math. With a million dollars in CDs paying 5% interest, you'd earn an annual income of $50,000 a year before taxes without ever touching the principle. After payroll and income taxes, that would leave you about $31,000 to spend on your million-dollar investment. (And that's assuming you have a million in the first place).

Option 5: There's One More Way: It's the path to solid, on-going income that successful authors, songwriters, musicians, actors, and performing artists follow. You produce work, usually in the form of intellectual property, that pays a pipeline of recurring income via royalties, also known as residual income or passive income. Unfortunately, very few of us have a bestselling book or record or a brilliant invention in us. Only a very elite group of gifted people has the God-given talent to become the next Thomas Edison or Stephen King.

But you know what? There is a way that you—whoever you are, whatever your sex or race or family background or social status… whatever your education or past history of success or failure in any endeavor—can begin to earn enduring, residual-like income right now, starting today!

It's called Network Marketing.

And before you say—or think—another thing, I want you to give me a chance... no—scratch that—I want YOU to make the chance FOR YOURSELF to take a look at Network Marketing and see what it has to offer you.

YOU'VE GOT EVERYTHING TO GAIN

In earlier chapters you learned how our entire world is filled with pyramids—good ones, bad ones, legal ones, and illegal ones. Doesn't the fact that all these businesses and social and cultural institutions—like schools, colleges, government, churches, and, yes, even families—are all multi-level pyramids tell you something interesting?

The fundamental structure or shape has nothing to do with an enterprise being "good" or "bad," does it? Rather, it's what people do with it—how they apply the natural pyramid principle of value flowing down in direct proportion to power (in the form of dollars or votes) flowing up that makes the difference.

What does that mean for you? Just this: How you make use of what's available to you is your choice.

And I believe the best possible option available to you today is Network Marketing.

I'm going to show you and tell you what Network Marketing *is*... and what it *is not*.

I want you to understand this business. I want you to compare it to all the other ways of earning a living we've talked about and see how it measures up.

I want you to look at Network Marketing and see if it will provide you the security and freedom you need to capture and keep your American Dream.

You've got little to lose. And if what I say about Network Marketing is true—think for just a moment about what you might have to gain!

Why Traditional Ways Don't Work Anymore

Chapter Eight

Paradigm—A $100 Word and a Million-Dollar Idea

When one door closes, another opens.
But we often look so long and
so regretfully upon the closed
door that we do not see the one
which has opened before us.
—Helen Keller

I'm sure you've heard the word "paradigm" before. It's one of those $100 college words that actually has a pretty simple meaning.

A paradigm is a point of view or a model, the way we see the world around us—"the way things are…" kind of like the status quo. The American Dream is a paradigm (only for most of us today, it's the way it was—not the way it is).

What follows is a good example of what paradigms are—and how they change.

THE SWISS WATCH PARADIGM

Do you remember what the gold standard was—the prevailing paradigm—for watch-making back in 1975? The Swiss watch, right? It was Rolex and the like, perfecting technology that dates back to the 14th century: classic, accurate, 31 jewels, a mainspring to wind up, tick-tick-tick-tick-tick….

Suddenly, one day, this little old Swiss watchmaker comes running out of his shop jumping up and down about this neat, new watch he'd just made.

"Look, Wolfgang—no mainspring, no jewels. It's lighter and a whole lot cheaper to make. It's thinner and you never have to wind it. And— it's a hundred times more accurate! It's called a quartz watch!"

Well, the Swiss are a pretty cautious and conservative bunch. So their first response was to lean back, puff on their pipes, and say,

"Hold on now, Fritz—not so fast. This quartz thing is pretty clever. But look, if we start making these quartz watches, then who's gonna want these big expensive 31-jewel jobs we make now? We'll be competing against ourselves. We've got millions invested in jewels and gears and springs and things. What are we going to do with all of that stuff—throw it away? And what are we going to do with all the little old watchmakers—like you? Besides, we own the watch business now. We're the kings of the mountain. Why mess with success? Let's not fix what's not broken."

The Swiss Watch Paradigm—that's the way it was.

See, the Swiss didn't think quartz technology would amount to much. So, instead of rocking their own boat, they sold the technology—to the Japanese.

You may remember the Japanese from the early 1950s—they were the guys who made all that cheap stuff that broke 10 minutes after you bought it.

"Made in Japan"—Ha ha ha!

Ha ha, indeed. Who owns the watch market now? The Japanese and Chinese and their quartz watches, that's who!

We didn't just change watches—we changed paradigms.

MOVE OVER, ROLEX—HERE COMES SEIKO

The last time the Swiss had a really big hit in the watch business was Swatch. Cheap, light, cute, bright—*and quartz*! They copied them from the Japanese!

See, a paradigm—the way it is—becomes "the way it was" when it doesn't work anymore. Or when somebody invents a new and improved paradigm to take its place.

Right now, for example, the old paradigm of the American Dream has stopped working for all but a very, very few.

We know that's true by answering one simple question: Have you gotten your slice of the American pie? Is it working for you? Are you living the American Dream right now?

If you're not, believe me, you're not alone. You're part of a mega-group that's been given a new definition of "middle" class— you're in the middle, all right, caught between a rock and a hard place!

Now, don't get caught in the trap of saying something like, "Well, I just don't work hard enough…" or, "I'm just not smart enough…."

Tell me the honest truth—if you worked twice as hard as you do now, would that really make a difference? Would you be earning twice as much? And do you really need to be twice as smart as you are right now to make it in this world—to be a success?

Look around: the "A" students are working for the "C" students. Being two or three times smarter isn't the answer, either. If intelligence were the answer, college professors would be the wealthiest people in the world—and we both know that's not the way it is.

If you're like most people I know, you probably believe the reason you don't have the American Dream is because you didn't take all the right steps you were supposed to take. You probably think you got off track somewhere—that you're missing something—and if you only had the missing ingredient, you'd have your Dream and be able to live it, too. Is that true?

Well, my friends, it's not your fault. You're not missing anything.

What's missing is a new American Dream paradigm—one that works. Because the old American Dream isn't around anymore. Why? *It's been stolen!*

WHO STOLE THE AMERICAN DREAM?

Wanna know who stole the American Dream? I'll tell you who stole the American Dream:

CEOs who are making hundreds of millions while their companies are laying off loyal workers by the thousands—that's who!

Giant Corporations that are eliminating pension plans for tens of thousands of workers while giving a handful of key managers back-dated stock options and retirement packages worth hundreds of millions—that's who!

Politicians who are voting themselves raises and perks and generous pension plans, all the while twiddling their thumbs and doing NOTHING about out-of-control Social Security and Medicare spending, which are threatening to bankrupt our country for generations—that's who!

Out-of-touch friends and relatives who keep telling you to trade your freedom for dependence on a job that probably won't be there in a few short years—that's who!

All-powerful mainstream media that pick through a barrel of good apples in the hopes of finding one bad apple so they can broadcast their negativity to the world—that's who!

Uninspired and timid teachers who brainwash students into thinking that the sole purpose of a good education is to get a good job—that's who!

Rich hedge fund managers who make themselves even richer by pressuring U.S. companies to ship good-paying jobs overseas—that's who!

Dozens of Fortune 1000 companies that make their profits from North American consumers yet transfer their corporate headquarters to a Caribbean island address to legally avoid paying federal income taxes—that's who!

Wal-Mart's "everyday low pricing," a ruthless business model that demands suppliers match the "China price," forcing more and more North American manufacturers to close factories in favor of cheap labor in Asia—that's who!

North American-based multi-national oil companies, who blame $3 a gallon gas on OPEC suppliers, yet are raking in record profits at the rate of *$100 MILLION A DAY*—that's who.

State and local unions who are bankrupting our cities by demanding excessive pensions and retirement benefits for their millions of members—that's who!

Washington lobbyists, almost 40,000 in number (including hundreds of ex-congressmen), who are buying our politicians and writing our laws—that's who!

The reason you and millions of others like you don't have the American Dream—and the reason I didn't used to have it, either—is that there are a bunch of greedy guys out there with a vested interest in lining their own pockets while perpetuating the old "get-a-good-job" myth.

The bosses and CEOs of the world know that as long as they can keep the average worker dependent upon them for a small weekly paycheck, the big money will keep rolling right on up to the top of the pyramid, right into their corner offices.

And the best way to do that is to make sure you don't get your fair share. Less for you, more for them, right?

Look, if you were king of the mountain, would you really want to rock the boat? Would you risk being the one on top just to try something new? Or would you be like the guys who owned the Swiss watch business and hold tight until that foolish quartz thing blew over?

Remember, people generally resist change. And the comfort zone is all the more comfortable when you're rich and famous—when you're the one who's king.

What Walt Disney was talking about when he said it took courage to pursue your dreams was having the courage to accept change— the courage to climb aboard a new and better idea before everybody else does... because if you wait 'til everyone is doing it—it's too late!

SUCCESSFUL PEOPLE SWIM UPSTREAM

The late Sam Walton's advice for success was to "swim upstream," as he put it. "If everybody else is doing it," Sam said, "there's a good chance you can find your niche by going in exactly the opposite direction."

Think about it: By the time regular people get into a hot real estate market… or by the time the stock market hits a new high, the big money has already been made, isn't that true? The experts are long gone and all that's left for the ordinary guys and gals are the crumbs.

Mark Twain, who unwisely invested in a string of unsuccessful business ventures, speaks for most of us when he said: *"I was seldom able to see an opportunity until it ceased to be one."*

The new and better paradigm I'm talking about—the way you can get back the American Dream—is not the college-and-a-career-track paradigm—like it used to be.

Not the job-with-corporate-America paradigm—like it used to be.

Not the start-a-small-business-from-scratch paradigm, either.

Believe me, I tried them all. And I didn't make it in any of them.

But I did make it in the new and better paradigm of Network Marketing.

College, corporate jobs, even small business ownership—they're all old paradigm stuff. Wind up Swiss watches. Dead and dying dinosaurs. It's time to swim upstream—or drown!

THE NEW AND BETTER IDEA OF NETWORK MARKETING

Network Marketing is the quartz watch of business today. Because Network Marketing has what's missing from conventional business.

And what's that?

In a word—*a better idea.*

And what's that mean?

A better idea is simply "a new and better and different way of doing something."

Better ideas swim upstream, to use Sam Walton's words.

Better ideas are the engine of change.

Better ideas shatter old paradigms… and create new paradigms.

Better ideas are often subversive… revolutionary… odd… unthinkable… even undoable (at least in the minds of conventional wisdom and the people running the old "tired and true" ideas).

But America (and the rest of the world is catching up quick) defined itself as the place where people could try new and better and different ideas and succeed, or fail, on the viability of their dreams.

America is rife with examples of better ideas that have transformed the way we live and work and shop, starting in the early 20th century with Henry Ford and his better idea to mass-produce cars on an assembly line.

Here are just a few better ideas that have transformed the way we live and work and shop in recent years:

Franchising—find a profitable business model with a proven, copycat system and then duplicate it in thousands of locations across the country and around the world.

Subway Sandwiches—enjoy a healthier alternative to fast-food franchises by offering sub sandwiches packed with fresh ingredients of your choosing.

The Home Depot—allow consumers to wander around a giant warehouse and take advantage of home improvement products and services at contractor prices.

Starbucks—open European-style coffee shops in every North American city before exporting the concept around the globe.

Dell—offer low-cost, custom-built PCs on line and have them delivered to the customer's door in less than a week.

FOX—start a new TV network that offers viewers an alternative to the Big Three networks and their liberal-dominated slant on the news.

Network Marketing—re-organize and re-energize the way products are marketed and distributed by replacing salaried middlemen and retailers with commission-only independent contractors.

All of these better ideas—these new and different ways of doing something—became wildly successful because they shattered old paradigms by delivering more value down the pyramid in exchange for money going back up.

Network Marketing offers consumers not only one-of-a-kind products and services at fair and reasonable prices, but also the opportunity for average people to create wealth for themselves and their families with a modest investment of money.

Yes, franchising was a *better idea*, with its proven, cookie-cutter system and corporate support.

But personal franchising—in the form of Network Marketing—is the *best idea* because it has all of the advantages of traditional franchising at a fraction of the up-front costs. Network Marketing—a brilliant idea whose time has come.

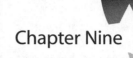

Chapter Nine

Why Network Marketing? Ch...Ch...Ch...Changes

*Change is the law of life. And those
who only look to the past or present
are certain to miss the future.*
—Pres. John F. Kennedy

C hange. It's the most fundamental fact of life in our world today.

But, as a rule, people are reluctant to change. We resist it. It has to do with staying in our comfort zone, which is part of human nature.

But it's also true that what you resist—persists. And when you push against a change whose time has come—it resists big time!

You more you resist change... the more change resists you!

ENLIGHTENMENT VS. 'EN-DARKENMENT'
Throughout human history, as changes have come to light, people have run around blowing out candles and throwing the switches, demanding continued darkness.

In every field of endeavor—the arts, sciences, medicine, business —most new ideas have met with resistance and rejection at first. And the more unique and revolutionary the idea, the more sweeping and vast the change, the louder and stronger people's opposition to it.

It's not hard to understand why frightened, superstitious people in the Dark Ages, or even in the 17th, 18th, and 19th centuries, were threatened by new paradigms. The authorities threw Copernicus in jail. Threatened Galileo. Ridiculed Christopher Columbus. Laughed at Louis Pasteur. Even mocked Edison and Einstein. And you know, even today, we still resist change.

Let's look at some recent examples.

THE BUYING AND SELLING OF AMERICA

Once upon a time, back in the 1700s through the early 1800s, North Americans bought what they needed at small, family-owned specialty shops.

It was the butcher, the baker, and the candlestick maker paradigm.

Then, an Irish immigrant named A.T. Stewart had a very bright idea. He decided to combine all these separate little shops under one roof in one big store. In 1862, he built what became known as "the Marble Palace" in New York City, a giant, multi-storied building where shoppers could buy everything they needed for their households just by walking from one "department" to another.

Department stores with now-famous names, such as Macy's… Lord & Taylor's… Sears… Woolworth's… Hudson's Bay Company… Marshall Field… Wannamaker's… and JCPenneys sprung up across the continent, and we entered the golden age of department stores.

Department stores offered consumers a new paradigm for shopping… a new and better way of doing things. More merchandise. Better pricing. Better quality. More convenience.

And people flocked to them. In 1900, as many as 40,000 shoppers a day would march through the aisles of Marshall Field in Chicago.

Can you guess what happened next?

MAKING MONEY THE OLD-FASHIONED WAY

The individual merchants who owned those mom-and-pop specialty stores were unhappy people, to say the least. They saw their business drop to next to nothing as more and more people sought the wider selection, lower prices, and greater convenience of the local department stores.

The small mom-and-pop outfits started dropping like flies.

Well, those shopkeepers didn't take it lying down—no sir! They fought back. However, they didn't fight back with a new and better idea themselves. Instead, they fought change by clinging to the old paradigm while fighting back politically.

Since there were thousands and thousands of shopkeepers (with thousands and thousands of votes), they lobbied hard and fast for their right to do things the same old way.

As we're all aware, protest lost out to progress, and department stores became the predominant shopping paradigm of the late 19th through the mid-20th centuries until the next new paradigm—the shopping mall—took a big chunk of their business.

Remember, *what you resist—persists*. You'd have better luck standing in front of an oncoming freight train than to fight against a change to a new and better way of doing things whose time has come— especially when consumers love the idea.

SHOPPING CENTERS AND MALLS

After the chain department stores took over the major market share in retailing—the smaller merchants finally came to their senses and embraced the new technology. They began to look for innovative ways to leverage the department store paradigm for themselves.

As the automobile made growing suburbs out of near-city farm land, groups of small merchants got together in a collective way and formed shopping centers—a variety of individual stores all in the same convenient location. The zoning battles that followed—fueled by all the shop owners who didn't get into the new shopping centers—were nasty indeed.

Eventually, shopping centers, too, proliferated. And before long, developers enclosed them and put roofs over them—kind of like what the chain department stores had done initially—and called them shopping "malls."

Malls quickly became a way of life in North America.

Yet today, both department stores and malls are becoming old and dying paradigms.

As futurist Faith Popcorn says in her best-selling book, *The Popcorn Report*:

"Like the corporation, the shopping experience as we know it has grown cumbersome, inefficient, a violation of trends. The big department stores are discovering that it's no longer possible to be all things to all customers. The shopping center is becoming a dinosaur in the grand scheme of things."

FIGHTING A LOSING BATTLE

No one—and no thing—is immune to change, including department stores, which are now losing the battle for consumers that they won a century ago.

What happened?

Monster malls… specialty shops… big-box discount stores… catalogs… and e-commerce sites are eating their lunch. Purchases at chain department stores have dropped nearly 50% since 1974, while the number of shoppers at discount stores was up 65% in the same period. Meanwhile, e-commerce continues to grow by leaps and bounds, further eroding department store sales.

Today, malls are facing the same fate as department stores—too many locations and not enough shoppers. So, to combat competition, developers are turning to Hollywood gimmicks to attract shoppers. Enter the mall as a theme park… shopping as entertainment. Check out Century City in L.A.—or even better, Canada's Edmonton Mall—the Disneyland of malls.

Edmonton Mall. Wow! A shopping mall that's 115 football fields in size and houses the world's largest indoor amusement park, indoor wave pool, and indoor miniature golf course! There's a fleet of operable submarines, a full-size replica of Christopher Columbus' ship, the *Santa Maria*, and—oh, yes—nearly 1,000 individual stores!

Know what's even more amazing?… the Mall of America in Bloomington, Minnesota, is even bigger! What's next—put a roof over the state of Rhode Island? How's that for power shopping?

But that's what it takes to make a mall that works today. Unfortunately, even a "Six-Flags-comes-to-the-mall" approach can't guarantee success—at last report, Edmonton Mall has lots of shuttered storefronts and empty parking spaces.

It's tough to compete when your paradigm is sinking.

FRANCHISING

One of the most amazing innovations in how America buys and sells what it wants was—and still is—franchising.

You know, 50 years ago franchising was a revolutionary new technology—a new and better way to retail goods, food products, and services to the consumer.

And boy, did people hate it! Resistance, big time.

Newspapers and magazines shouted bold headlines about what a scam and rip-off franchising was. Stories of little old ladies who lost their life savings to some flim-flam franchise were everywhere.

Even though some very big, well-known Fortune 500-type companies were involved in franchising, CEOs refused to allow their corporations to be used in ads or magazine stories—even about their own franchises! In fact, franchising actually came within 11 votes of being outlawed by Congress (sounds a little like the first department stores, doesn't it?).

Today—this once shaky, shady, so-called scam is responsible for over 33% of all retail sales in North America. Franchises sell nearly a trillion dollars of products a year from 1,000 different franchised concepts—and it's still growing! What will this figure be once franchising catches fire in China? Scary, isn't it?

Franchising was simply a new technology. Clearly, a revolutionary, very powerful, and very, very successful technology—a new and better and different idea for the distribution and sales of goods and services.

AN EVEN NEWER TECHNOLOGY OF DISTRIBUTION AND SALES

Is there a new next step in the evolution of our free enterprise system?

Is there a new, emerging distribution and sales technology on the horizon that'll out-perform franchising, the current king of retailing?

Yes, there is.

It's called Network Marketing.

And even more than department chains, big-box discount stores, shopping centers, malls, and franchising that came before, Network Marketing has been resisted. It's been misunderstood, criticized, laughed at, and lobbied and legislated against.

Just like department stores... just like franchising...

Who's laughing now?

THE PIONEERS

Direct Selling has a long, rich history in North America, dating back to the 1600s when "Yankee peddlers" would canvass city neighborhoods

71

and travel back roads from village to village peddling much-needed household wares, such as pots and pans, candles, and the like.

Then, in the late 1800s, Richard Sears, founder of Sears and Roebucks, installed the first formal Network Marketing compensation system by rewarding catalog customers with points that could be exchanged for merchandise or cash for referring friends and family members to Sears' mail order division.

In the early 1900s, an African-American woman named Madam CJ Walker laid the groundwork for modern Networking opportunities by recruiting ambitious but underemployed black women to sell her hair and skin products for commissions. The uneducated daughter of slaves, Walker quickly recognized that personal growth was essential to success, and she opened training centers in several cities to teach her reps strategies for success. By the time of her death in 1917, Walker's company employed 20,000 independent sales reps across North America. *The Guinness Book of World Records* cites Walker as the first American female self-made millionaire.

Mr. Sears and Madam Walker set the stage for Network Marketing by adopting unconventional approaches that would motivate everyday consumers to make money while making a difference in their lives and the lives of family and friends.

That's why I say the Network Marketing of the new millennium is such a powerful vehicle for financial independence—it has a history of continually reinventing itself by exploiting the latest technologies. As one industry observer puts it, "The future's so bright you gotta wear sunglasses!"

I'm convinced we will see history repeat itself here.

I'm convinced Network Marketing will surpass the astounding success of department stores and franchises… that Network Marketing will revolutionize the way North America and the world buys and sells everything!

Why? Look around.

It's already happening.

Chapter Ten

Whisper This Word to Yourself: 'Distribution'

*All too many men go through the
forest and see no firewood.*
—English proverb

In his breakthrough book, *Unlimited Wealth*, noted economist Paul Zane Pilzer asks the reader to recall a memorable scene from the 1960s iconic movie *The Graduate*. Dustin Hoffman plays the part of Ben, a recent college graduate who is clueless about what to do with his future. One evening at a party, an older, wiser man pulls Ben aside to share the secret to business in the years ahead. He whispers one word in Ben's ear:

"Plastics."

In *Unlimited Wealth*, Pilzer whispers a different, though no less profound and magical word, in our ears:

"Distribution."

Here's why.

THE TECHNOLOGY OF DISTRIBUTION

The most visible and powerful impact technology has had to date on the goods and services we buy is in reducing the cost of making a product. And it's a proven marketing law that when you lower the price, you sell much, much more. For example, few Americans owned calculators when they sold for $125. Once the retail price dropped below $20, everybody got one—and then two or three. The same was true for computers and cell phones and a whole range of products.

Just look at what happened to LCD and plasma TVs.

When it cost $5,000-plus for a flat-screen TV, only the rich people owned them. But when the prices started plunging to the $1,000 range, or cheaper, they started flying off the shelves. Today, you can buy a flat-screen, hi-definition plasma TV with remote for what it cost to buy a black and white console TV in the 1960s.

Pick a product—any product—and you'll find the same thing has happened. Adjust the dollars for inflation, and today you can buy six to seven times the value, quality, features, safety, and longevity than you could 20 years… or even 10 short years ago. Today you get a far better quality TV… or refrigerator… or microwave… or desktop music system… or laptop computer… and it costs 60% less yet has 10 times the features.

Advances in technology, that is, new and better ways of doing things (in this case, of making things) have slashed retail prices, and, as a result, more units get sold. When the price comes down, then what was once a luxury item suddenly becomes a necessity. Everybody has to have one… then two… then three (got to have one in the garage).

Today, 95% of homeowners have *at least* two TVs; the majority of homes have three or more TVs. Many upscale newly built homes have TVs projected through the bathroom mirror!

Once you have every room equipped with a TV or two, what's next?

Better quality.

That five-year-old 42-inch TV in the living room gets replaced by a 60-inch jobie complete with surround sound. And on and on it goes. Who wants a Sony Walkman now that video i-Pods are available? First comes quantity. Then comes quality. And since technology is constantly producing new and better ways of making things, as well as new and better things we never even thought of before—there are always new and better products for new and bigger markets.

That, my friends, is what makes America the leader of the world—and will keep them us there as long as all our credit cards aren't maxed out.

We are the world's biggest market for just about everything. They (the Chinese, the Japanese, the Germans, and any other of "they") may giggle behind our backs... make snide remarks about "materialistic Americans," but the laughing stops when the marketing begins. They know which side their bread is buttered on—and they know who's got the bread, baby!

BUT WHY DO SOME THINGS KEEP GOING UP IN PRICE?

Okay, if prices are dropping like autumn leaves in Maine, why is it that some prices haven't come down in price? Food, for example?

Great question—and food is a perfect example of prices that keep edging up. Here's why. The cost of growing food, such as wheat, and turning it into, say, cereal, was lowered to rock bottom by new and better growing and production technologies many years ago.

In a box of cereal, the cereal itself may cost 10 cents. If you improve farming and manufacturing 20%, you only knock 2 cents off the price of the food. So, why does Kellogg or Post charge $3.50 for the box of cereal? Because the biggest cost of the product isn't in the manufacturing. And it's not in the packaging, either, which adds only another dime. Other than marketing, the biggest cost is in something you can't see or taste.

The biggest cost is in the distribution and sales!

It used to be that a product's production cost was around 50% of the retail price. That was in the olden days. Advances in manufacturing technology—all the way from the cost of farming or mining the raw materials through producing the final product—has dropped the cost down to 10% to 20% max of the final retail price. With overcapacity in food production... and with China and India and Mexico and Vietnam and others manufacturing stuff for pennies instead of dollars, the "cost of goods" is about as low as it can go.

But while manufacturing costs were being slashed, the costs of distribution and sales were climbing higher and higher. Today, those expenses represent about 80% to 90% of what a consumer pays for a product.

Now, if you want to be the most competitive retailer with the lowest price, which are you going to do?

a) Focus your efforts on reducing the already rock-bottom cost of making a product to recapture a few pennies?

Or...
b) Concentrate on the 80% to 90% it costs to distribute and sell that product?

You'd choose "b)", of course.

Here's how a product priced at $1 would play out. Saving 10% to 20% off the 10-cent cost of production would put an extra 2 cents in your pocket, tops. Whereas by taking 20% out of the 80-cent to 90-cent cost of distribution and sales, you're looking at an extra 16 cents to 18 cents in gross profit. Multiply that 18 cents by millions of products sold, and we're looking at the difference between a healthy, high-profit enterprise versus surviving by the skin of your teeth.

Distribution—that's where the money is these days. If you need proof, just look at the richest family in America: the Walton's.

AMERICA'S REAL UNCLE SAM

The late Sam Walton's family owns Wal-Mart, easily the most successful distributor of merchandise in the world.

Just how successful is Wal-Mart?

When the four Walton heirs sit down for Sunday dinner, the collective net worth of the people at the table is $100 billion, give or take a couple of hundred million that might have dropped out of somebody's pocket on the way to Mom's house. If Daddy Sam were still alive, he'd be the richest man in the world, nearly doubling number two Bill Gates at $53 billion.

And what did "Uncle Sam" Walton and his Wal-Mart stores do to create this amazing mass of money?

Distribution.

Wal-Mart distributes and sells other people's products. In fact, they don't really sell anything. They just *make available* the best-selling models and brands as part of the widest selection in one convenient location at the absolute cheapest prices in town. How good are they at distribution? Here's a joke that's made the rounds: "How do you find the local Wal-Mart store? It's right across the street from the boarded-up Kmart."

Yep, they're that good. And getting better, moving into distributing groceries… and prescription drugs… and tires… and gasoline— and setting their sights on conquering China.

Distribution—that's the key!

If you can develop a new and better method—a better technology for distributing goods and services than most businesses are using today—you will be very, very rich tomorrow.

And the good news is you don't have to design and develop that new and better method of distribution and sales all by yourself. Because it's already here, up and working, right now. What's more, it has been successfully tested, refined, and proven in the marketplace for more than 50 years.

Today, *tens of thousands* of people are distributing *millions* of products worth *billions* of dollars in a 100 countries around the globe using the latest leading-edge technology that is revolutionizing the way people shop and receive products and services.

Instead of making the Walton family richer, these leading-edge distributors are making *their* families richer. And that's a new and better way of doing things that anyone can understand.

Chapter Eleven

The Biggest Edge

*Kodak sells film. But they
don't advertise film. They
advertise memories.*
—Theodore Levitt
educator

With millions of products available in the marketplace and with 3,000 to 5,000 advertisements bombarding us each day, advertisers need an edge to get their products to stand out from the thundering herd.

The edge—that's the Holy Grail of successful advertising.

Take this quick quiz to see if you can match the following well-known products with their advertising edges:

Product	Edge
1. Volvo ___	a. Lowest prices
2. Apple Computer ___	b. Sin and excitement
3. BMW ___	c. Superior driving experience
4. Las Vegas ___	d. Individualism
5. Wal-Mart ___	e. Safety
6. Tiffany Jewelry ___	f. Glamour and luxury

Answers: 1-e; 2-d; 3-c; 4-b; 5-a; 6-f

ADS AD NAUSEAM

The six products listed above have been around for decades, so their edge in the marketplace is firmly planted in the minds of consumers. But what about the other hundreds of thousands of products seeking buyers?... how are advertisers trying to get an edge amid all of the commercial clutter? The answer—by getting more creative—no, make that MORE DESPERATE—in the content and placement of their ads.

"Advertisers will not be satisfied until they put their mark on every blade of grass," quips Rance Crain, editor-in-chief of the trade magazine *Advertising Age*. Desperate to gain an edge, advertisers are pushing into areas of our lives that are annoying, if not downright disturbing.

Some samples. CBS laser-stamped 35,000 eggs with its famous eye logo. Public schools are not only pumping radio and TV ads into buses and classrooms, but they're also selling naming rights to athletic facilities and, gulp, even lunchrooms. U.S. Airways takes in nearly $10 million each year selling ads on tray tables and napkins and is negotiating to sell ads—I'm not making this up—on their airsickness bags! And Columbia Pictures signed an agreement to cover the bases at all Major League Baseball parks with Spider Man II logos. (Fortunately, irate fans revolted and the studio called it off).

The result of this mad scramble for an edge? Consumers are becoming immunized to the messages and even turned off by the messengers. When ads become too intrusive and violate our sense of decorum, we make sure to remember the product so we will be sure NOT to buy it.

So, how do savvy marketers get an edge by cutting through the clutter and impacting consumers with quality-over-quantity messages that resonate with sincerity rather than shock?

By employing the Biggest Edge—person-to person, face-to-face marketing, that's how. Which is why Network Marketing is booming like a Fourth of July fireworks display while the fuse on traditional marketing methods is fizzling out....

FACE TIME: THE BIGGEST EDGE

Most people assume that low prices are still the Biggest Edge in marketing.

Not true.

Yes, low prices, as Wal-Mart has proved, is a big edge. But having the lowest prices is NOT the Biggest Edge. If the lowest prices were the biggest edge, then every one would drive a Kia and eat at home, saving themselves thousands of dollars a year. But plenty of middle class people buy BMWs and dine at ritzy, high-priced restaurants. Why? Because people intuitively understand that the price of a product is measured in more than dollars and cents.

"Price is what you have to give up to get what you want," says marketing guru Dr. Bill Quain, author of the bestselling book, *Pro-sumer Power*. When you shop at Wal-Mart or Costco, posits Dr. Quain, you may pay less money than shopping elsewhere, but you GIVE UP tons of intangibles to get that low price. When you shop at Wal-Mart, just look at what you have to *give up* to get what you want:

You *give up* great service.

You *give up* beautiful surroundings.

You *give up* a friendly, knowledgeable sales person.

You *give up* luxury.

You *give up* top-quality, one-of-a-kind products.

In short, you *give up enjoying a pleasurable experience...* and in exchange, *you get to endure a miserable experience* to save a few cents on a tube of toothpaste. Thanks, but no thanks.

That's why I say the Biggest Edge isn't the lowest price. Not even close. The Biggest Edge today is the same as the Biggest Edge was 5,000 years ago... and the same as the Biggest Edge will be 5,000 years from now—one-on-one, person-to-person, face-to-face interaction with a knowledgeable representative.

That's the Biggest Edge. Always has been. Always will be.

THE CASE FOR FACE TO FACE

Several decades have passed since the publication of *Megatrends*, John Naisbitt's breakthrough bestseller that identified 10 new directions transforming our lives. Naisbitt was eerily accurate in predicting that person-to-person interaction would become increasingly important in the years ahead.

"High tech/high touch is a formula I use to describe the way we have responded to technology," Naisbitt wrote in 1982. "What happens is that whenever new technology is introduced into society, there must be a counterbalancing human response—that is, *high touch*. The more hi-tech, the more high touch."

The need for hi-touch explains why air travel is at an all-time high in an age when technology of cell phones, free long distance phone service, and instant messaging make communication faster, cheaper, and easier than ever before. Why would someone pay $500 to fly to a business meeting when they could video conference via the Internet for $5 or less? Because technology can enhance person-to-person relationships, but it can never REPLACE person-to-person interactions.

Recent research proves out Naisbitt's theory. Daniel Goleman, author of *Social Intelligence*, says that the human brain is wired for sociability. Goleman says that the "social brain" is active in human contact, but that it's inactive online, which explains why the Internet allows people to say things they would never say were they face to face.

"The quality of our relationships is under assault in modern life," Goleman asserts. "We need to remind ourselves more often to pay attention to the human moment... to put down the BlackBerry, turn off the cell phone, and pay attention to what's going on with the person you're interacting with."

Looking for the Biggest Edge? Then create hi-touch experiences with people, be they business associates, clients, customers, prospects, friends, relatives, children, spouses, or acquaintances. No amount of hi-tech can replace our in-born need for hi-touch, one human being relating to another human being face to face.

The Biggest Edge is a firm handshake... a confident smile... steady eye contact... active listening... a hearty laugh... a loving look... a pat on the back... a knowing nod... a hug of acceptance. Even in our Brave New Wired World, the need for hi-touch can never be duplicated. And never be digitized.

WELCOME TO THE HOSPITALITY ECONOMY

As recently as the 1970s, advertisers could reach 90% of the U.S. television audience just by buying ads on the three major networks at 9 p.m. Today's marketers have it tougher. Today's consumers expect more—a lot more!—than a 30-second commercial touting the features of their product.

"We are in a new business era," says Danny Meyer, author of *Setting the Table* and owner of 11 successful restaurants in New York City. "This is now a hospitality economy, no longer the service era. Service is the delivery of a product. Hospitality is how the delivery of a product *makes its recipient feel.*"

Network Marketing, with its emphasis on person-to-person presentations and mentoring, is the epitome of the hospitality economy. Networkers make people *feel* special. *Feel* energized. *Feel* hopeful. *Feel* engaged. And, well, *feel* human again.

While traditional marketers are staying up nights thinking of ways to shock viewers while losing market share, Network Marketers are shaking hands and making friends and recruiting new business partners.

Network Marketing offers average, everyday people the ultimate hospitality—access to one-of-a-kind, leading-edge products and services, plus the opportunity to own their own lives by owning their own low-cost, potentially high-profit (and hi-touch) business.

Now that you understand why Network Marketing lays claim to the Biggest Edge, let's turn the page to discover what Networking is and how it works.

The Truth
About
Network
Marketing

PHASE **4**

Chapter Twelve

What Is Network Marketing & How Does It Work?

We have lived through the age of
big industry and the age of the giant
corporation. But I believe this is
the age of the entrepreneur.
—Pres. Ronald Reagan

t really used to bother me when someone would say, "Network Marketing is a
pyramid scheme." I mean, look at what
we've revealed so far about our government, corporate America,
colleges and universities—all those good old "legal pyramid schemes"
that are ripping people off in a big way and getting away with it.

Sure, Network Marketing is a multi-level pyramid. But remember, everything that distributes goods and services is a pyramid. What
matters is whether value flows down through the levels of the pyramid
in direct proportion to the dollars that flow back up. Consumers need
to end up with a quality product or service, at a reasonable price—that's
bona fide distribution.

THE 80 – 20 RULE

Now, I'm not saying Network Marketing is pure and perfect. People
fail in this business, too. Just like they fail in school or drop out of
college. And by the way, look at the world—do you see more people
failing or succeeding?

The 80 – 20 rule applies to Network Marketing—just as it applies
to real estate sales and government jobs and everything else: 20% of the
people do 80% of the work and rightfully earn 80% of the profits.

It's absolutely true that Networking companies make mistakes... some even do downright stupid things. Some products don't cut it in the marketplace. When the value stops flowing down, any pyramid collapses—legal or illegal. And yes, there have been people who abuse the concept and make it dirty.

Sadly, there are Ken Lays and Bernie Ebberses in every business. It's the same with anything—and yes, Network Marketing, too.

You see, when it's all said and done, Network Marketing is quite an unconventional approach to distribution and sales. That's why the timing couldn't be better to become involved right now. And that doesn't sit well with people who've got their hearts and minds—and wallets—heavily invested in keeping the status quo—the same old conventional "Swiss watch" paradigm of doing things.

But keep in mind the late Sam Walton's advice: "When everyone else is floating downstream, swim upstream." You think the guys in the vinyl record business had great things to say about compact disc technology when they first saw it? If you want to catch major flak in this world, go out and do something in a new and better way—then duck! Nay-sayers are everywhere. (I wonder who pays those guys!)

THE POWER OF THE PYRAMID

Just for fun, take out a U.S. one dollar bill. Turn it over. Look at the left-hand side. What do you see? *A pyramid*!

The founders of our country recognized the pyramid as a strong, enduring structure. According to geometry, pyramids are strongest of all. Wide at the bottom and growing narrower at the top—able to support great weight and stand for ages against the natural elements.

The Founding Fathers of our nation were Freemasons, a brotherhood of builders. And in this case, a group of nation-builders who created the world's first real democracy founded on the principles of equal opportunity, freedom of choice, freedom of speech, and free enterprise.

The Latin mottos above and below the pyramid say: *Annuit Coeptis*, which means, "God has favored our undertaking." And, *Novus Ordo Seclorum*, which means, "A new order of the ages."

Interesting, isn't it? The United States of America, the pinnacle of free enterprise, is represented by a pyramid! And if ever there was a pure and perfect, democratic example of the best of free enterprise, it's Network Marketing.

THE POWER OF NETWORKING—CHRISTIANITY

Perhaps the most extraordinary example of the power of Networking is Christianity.

About 2000 years ago, Jesus Christ appeared with a compelling message about a new and better way of doing things. He gathered around him a small core group of people—average folks: fishermen, tax collectors, teenagers, and the like—who caught the vision, who shared His dream. He spoke to individuals, small groups, and large gatherings. The word spread.

Yet even among His ardent believers and followers, there was one who betrayed Him and others who denied and doubted, too. But no matter, for Jesus had taken a stand for a new way of living that was unshakable. It was such a powerful commitment that it extended long after He physically left this earth.

Now, almost 2,000 years later, that handful of believers has conveyed the message of Jesus Christ by word of mouth down through centuries to vastly more people than that small, original group probably ever dreamed possible—today more than 25% of the population on this planet are Christians... that's well over a billion people—and growing!

The spread of Christianity throughout the world was accomplished by many of the same principles we find operating today in Network Marketing: word-of-mouth or person-to-person recommendations... testimonials... enthusiastic sharing... caring for the success of others... recognition, friendship, partnership, and much more.

Christianity is a perfect example of the awesome power of Networking.

HOW NETWORK MARKETING WORKS

The Network Marketing business model is brilliant in its simplicity and effectiveness. Here's what happens:

A Network Marketing company manufactures or agrees to distribute a product or service. The company enters into partnerships with a network of independent distributors, each one in business for himself or herself. The company handles all the research and development, finance, management, public relations, warehousing, production, packaging, quality control, administration, shipping, data processing, and so on... and the company pays commission checks to all the distributors.

The distributors, in turn, market the products for the company.

Advertising executives will tell you that as much as 80% of the cost of getting a product to consumers today is the result of marketing expenses. According to *USA Today*, marketers will spend a record $270 BILLION on ads in major media and direct mail, with billions more earmarked in the near future for the "new frontier of advertising"— small screen devices, such as i-Pods, cell phones, laptops, BlackBerries, and video games. (That's why Network Marketing companies pay their distributors so well—instead of advertising widely in the media, they set aside that money for the independent distributors in the form of commissions and bonuses.)

From the money saved on advertising, Networking companies can offer their distributors the support they need to market the products—online order consolidation sites, online information and education, brochures, flyers, etc. Companies even provide training in how to grow the business.

The distributors' jobs are to move as much product as they can through an independent network of distributors—large or small— because distributors get paid on every product distributed through their organization. Since the individual distributors can personally sell only a small volume of products, they recruit other like-minded people to join them in their business. As an incentive to build big networks, distributors can earn a percentage of the volume of their entire organization.

Earning a small percentage of a big network translates to big bucks—and that's one of the powerful advantages Network Marketers and their companies have over more traditional direct-selling methods.

LOTS DOING A LITTLE

Success in traditional direct sales depends upon a few super salespeople who can each move a mountain of product. Network Marketing, on the other hand, is just the opposite. Success in this industry depends on a lot of people doing a little bit each.

Network Marketers build a network of independent distributors, each of whom owns his or her own Network Marketing business distributing products and building their own network of distributors.

No matter when you join a network organization, you are always the head of your own company... at the top of the pyramid, so to speak. Unlike conventional corporations with one chief executive at the top, in Network Marketing, everyone is the CEO of his or her own independent organization. It's literally a network of CEOs.

THE COMPANY WINS, TOO

Now, the Network Marketing company has done something pretty brilliant here. They've slashed a huge amount of money from their costs of distribution and sales. (Remember, as much as 80% of a product's cost comes from marketing.)

In effect, the company creates a partnership with their distributors whereby the corporation provides everything from the product to the promotional material—in exchange for the distributors' marketing efforts. And the company gets rewarded, too—by reducing overhead and eliminating many of the conventional costs of doing business.

The company has no more need to pay for an in-house sales force—and they eliminate all the costs of the sales force's offices, support staff, phones, cars, travel, and entertainment.

The company doesn't have to advertise anymore either, unless they choose to spread brand recognition. The distributors do the lion's share of advertising by way the most powerful advertising force of all time— word of mouth. Personal endorsements are the best way to educate and inform consumers about special products—which is the main reason you'll find some of the most unique, technically advanced, superior quality products in the world offered through Network Marketing.

The company doesn't employ—or pay salaries and benefits for—jobbers, wholesalers, brokers, store managers, clerks—all those middlemen who keep sticking their fingers in the profit pie. Since the Network Marketing company has no need for those jobs, they've got a ton of money "left over" to pay the independent distributors who are moving the products.

It's simple—brilliantly simple!

There's no big mystery to Network Marketing. It's just another form of marketing and distribution.

A new and better form? You be the judge.

DUPLICATION—HOW NETWORK MARKETING DISTRIBUTORS BUILD THEIR BUSINESSES

Have you ever heard of the doubling concept?

The word "duplicate" originally meant to double, and this concept of doubling is one of the most powerful forces in wealth creation and Network Marketing. To understand how the doubling concept works, put yourself in the following scenario:

If I offered you a million dollars cash, this very minute—or, if I offered to give you a penny doubled every day for a month… which would you choose?

If you're like most people, you'd probably choose the million dollars. But take my advice—don't do it. Instead, take the penny doubled.

Why? Because the doubling concept is sneaky powerful. Check this out:

At first glance, a penny doubled every day for a month doesn't sound like much, and, frankly, it doesn't look like much in the beginning, either.

After five days, you'd have all of 16 cents.

After 15 days, you have a whopping $163.84.

Doesn't look very promising, does it? (If you're beginning to regret taking my advice, hold on, there's more.)

On day 19, you'd have $2,621. Six days later, day 25—just 5 days before the end of the month—you'd have just over $167,000. Now, this is where it gets interesting. The next day your money would double to $335,000. The next, more than $671,000. The next—the 28th day— you'd have over $1,340,000. And two days later, on the 30th—the last day of the month—you'd have a grand total of $5,368,709.12! That's over $5 million! (And if you were lucky enough to choose one of the months with 31 days, you'd have close to $11 MILLION!).

All from one penny, which simply doubled every day.

This doubling principle is the way a business grows in Network Marketing—and it has made Networking the fastest method of expansion in the history of free enterprise.

Networking is compassionate capitalism on steroids!

JUST ONE PERSON A MONTH CAN MAKE YOU RICH

You know, McDonald's didn't start off with 10,000 restaurants all over the world. They started with just one. And that's just how you can start in Network Marketing—you plus one other person.

Do you think it would be possible for you to find just one person each month to join your business? Just one partner who's interested in more freedom, recognition, happiness, and security… one partner who's interested in improving the lives of his or her family?

One good person a month—that's all it takes!

And once you "sponsor" that person into the business with you, you become their coach—a teacher. Which means you don't need to concentrate all of your efforts on selling the products. You need to teach, coach, and mentor others.

Now, in month two, you teach your first new partner how to sponsor one other person, while you sponsor another new person. So, at the end of month two, you've personally sponsored two people and your first partner has sponsored one, as well. Now you've got a group of four—you and three others.

You do the same for month three, four, five, and so on.

At the end of your first year, you'll have personally sponsored only 12 people—one each month. And each one of them will have sponsored one person each month, as well… and so on and so on. The true art of Networking, the awesome power of the doubling concept, is that by teaching each person how to sponsor and teach only one person a month, *at the end of the year you would have 4,096 people in your organization!*

WORST-CASE SCENARIO IS STILL GREAT!

Now, that's in a perfect world—and you know we don't live in a perfect world. Remember Murphy's Law: "Whatever can go wrong, will go wrong."

Let's say that 80% of your distributors are no longer selling products (as I pointed out earlier, 80% of all businesses fail in the first year). But all is not lost. These former sellers have now become consumers—so even though they've stopped working the business, you're still getting paid commissions on their reorders. (So, even if they're not working their business, they're contributing to the bottom line of YOUR business. What a deal!).

Now let's take it one step further… let's assume the worst of the worst… let's assume 9 out of every 10 people you sponsor quit. To make matters worse, let's assume 90% of your entire group quits. Pretty bad news—don't you think? In a traditional business, you'd be in deep trouble.

But this is the non-traditional business of Network Marketing, so look again: You still have 10% of your organization left… 10% of 4,096 people—that's over 400 people in your organization. And each one of them is bringing in new people and teaching them to do the business, just like you.

Now, each one of these 400 people is using and selling products. Remember, that's how Network Marketers get paid—on the sales of products moved through their networks. So, if each person in your organization is moving $100 or $1000 worth of products each month, that's a total product volume of between $40,000 and $400,000 a month!

Here comes the exciting part—the company pays the distributors a percentage of that sales volume. If the Network Marketing company pays a 5% sales commission on your downline volume, you would be earning somewhere between $2,000 to $20,000 *per month*.

Now you understand the power of Network Marketing.

Now, let's talk a little history.

NETWORK MARKETING BECOMES A SENIOR CITIZEN

In the early 1940s, a company called California Vitamins discovered that all their new sales reps started out as satisfied customers first and that most of the reps' new customers came from friends and family. The company also discovered that it was easier to get a lot of people to sell a little product than it was to find those few superstars who could sell a whole lot all by themselves.

So, the company wisely combined those two ideas and designed a marketing and compensation structure that encouraged their sales reps to recruit new distributors from the ranks of satisfied customers, most of whom were family and friends. And then the company rewarded the sales staff by giving them a percentage of the sales produced by their entire group. The result was staggering: Even though each individual in a distributor network sold only a couple hundred dollars' worth of products, the whole group moved tens of thousands of dollars' worth of vitamins.

Modern-day Network Marketing was born.

Where is Network Marketing today? It's come a long way, baby!

Right now there are thousands of Network Marketing companies operating in the United States and Canada, Mexico, South America, the United Kingdom, Europe, Australia, New Zealand, Israel, Japan, and the Pacific Rim. Why, little Malaysia alone has more than 800 active Network Marketing companies!

WHAT KIND OF COMPANIES ARE INVOLVED IN NETWORK MARKETING?

Network Marketing is reported to be a $100 billion international industry, made up of Fortune 500 and New York Stock Exchange (NYSE) companies. Warren Buffett, the world's second richest man, owns three Networking companies. Household products giant Colgate-Palmolive has several successful Network Marketing subsidiaries.

Network Marketing companies have a 50-year history of innovation—and it shows in their product lines, which often feature leading-edge, hi-tech products and services. For example, Network Marketing companies led the way with environmentally safe products with no additives and no preservatives... pesticide-free, biodegradable products and packaging... and products made without animal testing—years before any of these became popular marketing trends.

In fact, Network Marketing companies have pioneered entire industries: energy drinks... weight-loss products and systems... healthy snacks... natural vitamin and mineral supplements... water purification devices... and concentrated, environmentally friendly household cleaners and detergents, to name a few.

Now that Network Marketing is gaining worldwide acceptance, more and more products are being offered through this dynamic industry. Today, you can buy at wholesale virtually any product you can find in a store—the variety of products and services is nearly endless. From groceries to automobiles... long distance phone services to sports equipment... personal development tapes and tools to discount travel services.

The list is nearly endless—and growing!

WHAT KIND OF PEOPLE ARE INVOLVED IN NETWORK MARKETING?

People just like you and me. All kinds of people from every conceivable walk of life, from bank presidents... to house painters... to homemakers... to contractors... to chiropractors... to comedians... to engineers... to police officers... to janitors... to financial planners... to retirees on fixed incomes... to retirees sailing the world on yachts... to everything in between.

In Network Marketing, it's not where you start that counts, but where you end, and if you are open to new ideas, positive, and are teachable, you could end up owning your own high-profit business and calling your own shots, no matter where you started.

COOPERATION VS. COMPETITION

One of the big reasons for the success of Network Marketing is that it's based on cooperation—not competition. Unlike traditional business, career advancement in Network Marketing comes directly from your helping to create success for all the people in your group, in your company, and in the industry as a whole.

It's much like the story of the woman who died and suddenly found herself at St. Peter's gate. She asked him to show her the difference between Heaven and Hell.

St. Peter took her to Hell, where she saw an endless banquet table set with the most abundant spread of magnificent, mouth-watering food and drink she'd ever seen! Yet the people seated at the table were all shrieking and crying, pulling at their hair, and tearing their clothes to rags. She had never seen such horrible pain and anguish.

She was about to ask St. Peter why—in the face of such delicious abundance—the people were so miserable. But as she glanced around, she discovered the answer for herself. All their eating utensils were three feet long! None of the people at the table could even get a taste of the luscious feast.

When she arrived in Heaven, she was surprised to find the exact same scene... the same endless table, the same fantastic food and drink—even the same three-foot-long forks and spoons. But here, everybody was happy and laughing, having a wonderful time.

"I don't get it... why is everyone so happy here?" she wondered out loud.

"Because here in Heaven," St. Peter whispered, "they reach across the table and feed each other."

Cooperation instead of competition is a powerful reason that more and more people are attracted to the Network Marketing concept. In fact, the best word I can think of to describe Networking has become a business buzz word—empowerment. And Network Marketing is the most empowering business of all!

WHY ARE PEOPLE INVOLVED IN NETWORK MARKETING?

People are involved in Network Marketing because they have a burning desire for a better way to live and work.

They're involved because they want to set their own schedules and be their own bosses.

They're involved because they want to help themselves succeed by helping others succeed.

They're involved because they dared to dream their dreams could come true.

They're involved because they had the guts and drive to do something to change their circumstances for the better.

They're involved because they're passionate about being paid what they're really worth, instead of what the job is worth.

They're involved because somebody cared enough about them to show them the awesome opportunity of Network Marketing.

And they're involved because they were ready to make a change.

THE FUTURE IS NOW

Folks, here's the truth: Network Marketing is in your future. One way or the other you will be involved. How you are involved is up to you—nobody else. You're either going to be spending money, buying products—and lots of them—from Network Marketers. Or you're going to be selling products and building an organization—and making money.

It's your choice.

Ask yourself, "Would I rather be the one spending the money… or the one making the money?"

The truth is, we can't live on two incomes today the way our parents did on one! It's a new world. For the first time in America's history, there's a whole generation of workers who are financially worse off than their parents were at the same age.

Remember, less than one half of one percent of all North Americans earns $100,000 a year or more. And if you want to be one of them, you're going to have to do something new and different.

NETWORK MARKETING—THE NEW WAY TO FINANCIAL FREEDOM

You'll never create real and lasting wealth trading time for money. Even the doctors, lawyers, and Indian chiefs can't do it anymore—and if the high-priced college grads can't cut it, how can you?

In Network Marketing you can break out of the time-for-money trap.

Passive income… recurring income… is where it's at. How many self-employed people do you know who could take off for a month and come back to a bigger paycheck than when they left? In fact, how many self-employed people could come back and find their business in one piece?

In Network Marketing, you could do just that. I've known a number of Network Marketers who left for a honeymoon or an extended vacation… and returned to find an even bigger check waiting for them than when they left! That's the power of passive income!

If you're a woman… if you're black, Hispanic, or any other minority… or if you're one of those people without a specialized, professional university degree—both the corporate world and the professional world are generally closed to you.

Not Network Marketing—it's wide open. No glass ceiling—in fact, there's not any kind of ceiling. You're free.

Look, I'm no different from you. I'm no smarter. I went to college and didn't learn how to become financially independent. I've had jobs, people telling me what to do… punching a clock… fighting traffic… running to keep up with the pack in the rat race.

I was making $5.50 an hour building boats. I waited on tables—gettin' nowhere in a hurry. I've had my own business, too. I got out just in time and only lost $200,000-plus!

But today, because of my involvement in the Network Marketing industry, I'm financially free. Can you say the same?

If you're willing to work… if you're teachable… and if you have a burning desire to become successful, then, yes—you can make it in Network Marketing.

ARE YOU READY?

Johnny Carson once said:

"Talent alone won't make you a success. Neither will being at the right place at the right time, unless you are ready. The most important question is: *'Are you ready?'*"

Right here—right now is the right time and the right place for Network Marketing.

It's interesting how resistant we are to change. Even when the handwriting is all over the wall—and the ceiling… and the floors—we still want to stay in our comfort zones—even when we're the most uncomfortable. Even when we're miserable.

Let's not sugar coat it. For things to change, you have to change. For things to get better, you have to get better.

You can blame your parents, your boss, the government, anyone, and everyone. But one simple fact remains: When it becomes harder to suffer than change, you will change!

Like the Chinese say, "If you don't change your direction—you're bound to end up where you're headed."

Be honest with yourself—do you like the direction you're headed in your life and career? Perhaps now is the time for a change. Perhaps now is the time to take a closer look at Network Marketing.

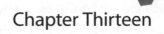

Chapter Thirteen

If Network Marketing Is So Great—Why Haven't We Been Told the Truth About It?

*My interest is in the future
because I'm going to spend
the rest of my life there.*
—Charles F. Kettering
American inventor

Why haven't we been told the truth about Network Marketing?

Because the world is filled with not-so-wise, dishonest people—shortsighted men and women who have yet to discover that, in hurting others, they hurt themselves most of all.

Remember the subtitle of this book?

"The book your boss doesn't want you to read."

Why would I say that?

Because it's not in your boss' best interest for you to learn there's a new and better way to live and work—a way that doesn't include the 9-to-5, trading-time-for-money insecurity trap of having someone else own your life... someone in command of the two words that stand between you and the street—"YOU'RE FIRED!"

There are lots of "know-it-all" bosses out there—lots of them! And it's not just your boss at work I'm talking about. It's all the self-proclaimed "bosses" in government, education, business, your neighborhood, or family, etc., who think they know what's best for you and me. Is it really your best interest they're looking out for… or their own?

POWER TO THE PEOPLE

The truth is that most of the people in power today are scared to death. Their overriding concern is the fear of loss—loss of their own power! Everywhere they turn, they see the handwriting on the wall—and they don't like the message. So what do they do?

They shoot the messenger.

Well, Network Marketing's message is "power to ALL the people"—not "power only to the bosses."

We've come a long way since the 1960s. Remember the anti-establishment movement? How so many of us wanted to change the way the world worked? Well, one reason that "revolution" didn't work was because we were spoiled and inexperienced and were better at whining and tearing down than building new and better ways of doing things to replace the old paradigms.

That was then… this is now. And now we do have a new and better paradigm for living and working.

IGNORANCE AND FEAR—A DEADLY COMBINATION

That's why more and more Network Marketing companies are wearing bullet-proof vests.

Remember how the Romans treated the Christians? They fed them to the lions!

Remember what the power-people did with franchising in the beginning? They called it a scam and a scheme. They were threatened by the message, so they tried to shoot the messenger full of holes.

It reminds me of the story about the first time a movie was shown in a Colorado mining town in the early 1900s. When the villain started threatening the heroine, a prospector jumped to his feet and shot the movie screen full of holes.

Sorry, "pahd-nah"—wrong tactic… and wrong target.

The movie just kept on playing.

SHOOT THE VILLAIN

Like the ignorant prospector, the media powers want to shoot the villain, too. After all, slaying villains attracts viewers and sells newspapers (and if the media can't find a villain, they create one).

As I mentioned earlier, in the 1950s and early '60s, a big media villain was the then-fledgling industry of franchising. To better understand why you haven't been told the truth about Network Marketing, let's take a brief look at how the media and its old paradigm partners—department stores and retail chains—ganged up on a new and better distribution method called franchising.

Back in the early days of franchising, when someone complained about losing money in a franchise, the media searched for all the dirty stories about franchising they could find. Blew the stories up bigger than life and tried to take franchising down.

Why?

Because the old, established department stores and chains were kings of the mountain, spending tons of money on TV, radio, and newspaper ads—and no one was in any hurry to put the cash cow on a diet. So, the media ran negative stories and the department store honchos got on their phones (and got out their checkbooks) to persuade their congressmen to pass legislation that would stop these upstart franchises dead in their tracks.

Came within a handful of votes of making it happen, too.

But in the end, new and better ways always triumph, and today, franchises account for 33% of the goods and services sold in North America.

MONEY IS SERIOUS BUSINESS

The media would have you believe they aren't about the money... that they're about truth and justice.

All I know is, if someone tells you it's not about the money, rest assured—it's about the money!

How many millions of dollars of advertising space do you think those early franchises were buying—compared to all the advertising bought by huge department stores and national chains that the franchises threatened with their new and better way?

Newspapers, magazines, radio, and television do not make a profit on readers, subscribers, listeners, and viewers. The media make money from their advertisers. BIG money. Outrageous money! And if you're not one of those big-ticket advertisers—you don't get the positive press coverage you need, much less deserve. Why should you? You're not making the media any money.

. What's more—what if you're some upstart competitive marketer taking sales and profits away from those free-spending advertisers with billion-dollar marketing budgets?

Do you really think Woolworth's and Grants, with their bustling lunch-counter business, were thrilled to death at Ray Kroc and his McDonald's? Once McDonald's got big enough to start taking market share away from those guys—and all the other established restaurants that advertised heavily in newspapers, radio, and TV... it was war!

Guess whose side the media was on?

Hey, even Fortune 500 companies who owned and invested in the franchise concept were afraid of telling the public they were involved. In the boardrooms they whispered, "Play it safe. If this franchise thing goes bust—nobody will know we blew it."

Courage, guys.

So, behind the scenes, the movement to stomp out franchising gained steam:

- Retailers put the pressure on the media... (They were losing sales)
- Manufacturers put the pressure on the retailers... (So were they)
- Media put the pressure on the public... (Their advertisers were being hurt—and the new guys weren't spending anywhere near what the good old boys were spending in advertising)
- Politicians, lobbied by big-payroll employers with big blocs of votes and even bigger campaign contributions, put the pressure on state and federal legislatures.

Together, they did their best to pass laws against franchising, declaring it illegal!

IT'S A MIRACLE FRANCHISING SURVIVED

Franchising not only survived—it prospered—because it was a new and better way of doing things… and because what you resist—persists. Today, more than one-third of everything we buy, both goods and services, comes from franchises—McDonald's, Dunkin' Donuts, Jazzercise, Mail Boxes Etc., Holiday Inn, and on and on—approaching $1 trillion in annual revenues worldwide—and still growing in double digits!!!

Do you see any more nasty newspaper articles today attacking franchising? Any more TV exposés on *20/20*? Nope. What you see and hear today are franchise slogans burned into our cultural consciousness:

"You deserve a break today."

"Where's the beef?"

Can you name one industry that does more advertising today—in newspapers, magazines, radio, and TV—than franchising?

And with all the money the franchising industry makes… and with the tremendous number of people employed by franchises across North America… and with the awesome contribution franchises make to federal, state, and local economies… and with the taxes they generate and all the votes they buy… how happy and cooperative are the politicians and media about the franchise industry now?

Folks, money talks… and you know what walks.

ALL ABOARD!

Let's face it—the story I just told you about franchising's early struggle for acceptance parallels the emergence of Network Marketing.

Networking companies spend pennies advertising compared to marketing budgets of traditional retailers, e-commerce sites, and franchises. And the old media of TV, radio, and print… and the new media of the Internet and hand-held devices don't like it one little bit.

To make matters worse, Network Marketing is getting "too big for our britches"—in other words, we're succeeding in the marketplace of the free enterprise system, big time. After all, worldwide, there are millions of Network Marketers… and tens of millions of satisfied customers… and billions of dollars' worth of products sold every year through Network Marketing!

And that's even harder for the "giant" corporations and big-box retailers to take because they've got the sneaking suspicion we just may be right... we may really be the wave of the future... we may really have managed to put the freedom they stole back into free enterprise.

THE ECONOMICS OF COMPETITION

Now, if you were sitting around the conference room in one of those traditional Goliath companies and your sales were slipping away—being stolen from you by a fast-growing Network Marketing company you simply couldn't compete with—what would you do?

Or if you were one of the brokers, retailers, wholesalers, media people, truckers, or any of the other people whose jobs or businesses were being threatened with extinction because Network Marketing was a new and better way of doing things—what would you do?

Well, if you had a friend in the state attorney general's office—you'd make a call, wouldn't you? And if you'd been contributing a bunch of money to an industry lobbyist or a political action committee, you'd call them too, wouldn't you?

In fact, if your job were on the line—either as the VP of sales or one of the executive staff who sooner or later had to answer to stockholders and explain why your market share was being taken away by some kooky "pyramid scheme"—you'd grab any strategy you could get your hands on and fight back—wouldn't you?

Remember, your future is at stake here... your position, your power—your paycheck!

BULLIES ON THE BEACH

Look, like I told you earlier, I'm not here to champion any particular Network Marketing company. My commitment is to the industry... to free enterprise itself... and to you! But I'll guarantee you this—you won't catch me cringing and biting my nails behind a palm tree while the bullies take over the beach!

One thing about bullies, though—they never fight fair. They always have their gang around to back them up in case the tide turns against them. And the biggest, baddest member of the corporate America gang is the media.

106

If life were a hockey game, the media would be the enforcer (he's called the "goon" in hockey lore). The goon's job is to intimidate the opposition. He patrols the ice like the Terminator, and first chance he gets, he throws down his hockey stick and starts serving up knuckle sandwiches.

THE MEDIA—CORPORATE AMERICA'S 'GOONS'

Well, the media are the "goons" for big business. When some Network Marketing competitor comes along and starts scoring points in the marketplace, the media send in the goons to cut 'em down to size. Traditional companies pay the media big bucks via advertising dollars... so, they send out their goons to protect their interests... and everybody's happy as a clam. Except the Networking company, who's been blindsided and knocked silly.

That's why every now and then you'll see an exposé on TV attacking a Networking company or a successful distributor. It just means the goon has been called into the game again... and he's gonna restore the peace by jacking some jaws.

When was the last time you saw an exposé on a corporate giant that spends hundreds of millions every year on TV advertising... companies like McDonald's? Or Pepsi? Or Nike? Never!

I have yet to see an exposé on ABC, NBC, CBS—or cable TV, for that matter—on the lawsuit that cost Metropolitan Life Insurance Co. $100 million for misleading sales tactics. Or an exposé on John Hancock Mutual Life Insurance Co. settling with 3.8 million policyholders for $600 million. Or an exposé on Prudential Insurance Co. of America's plan to pay $3.8 billion to settle a sales fraud lawsuit. Or an exposé on the $50 million fine against the makers of Bayer aspirin for price fixing.

Do you know why? Ever hear the expression, "Don't bite the hand that feeds you"? What happened to fair play? You don't have to be Sherlock Holmes to solve this one.

As far as the media are concerned, it's always been open season on Network Marketing companies and their top distributors... while "mum's the word" when big TV advertisers are caught with their hands in the cookie jar. It's happened before (and believe me, it will happen again).

107

DO YOUR HOMEWORK

Now, let's get one thing straight. Just as there are scams and schemes in any industry, there are a few Network Marketing companies that are blatantly illegal. There are good and bad apples in every industry, aren't there? Real estate has its swamp land scams... banking has its savings and loan crooks... the stock market has its insider-trading scandals... and so on.

So why should people expect Network Marketing to be any different?

It's a fact of life today that you can't be too trusting or naive. So open your eyes and ears. Do your homework. Check out the products... the people... the company... everything! So you know what you're getting into. That's good advice whether you're walking down a dark street... investing in the stock market... or getting started in a new business.

ANOTHER THING ABOUT ADVERTISING

Years ago, John Wanamaker, the legendary founder of one of the oldest department store chains in this country, said:

"I estimate 50% of my advertising is wasted—I just don't know which half!"

But that fact is lost on the Big Boys running corporate America. Advertising and media analysts estimate that advertising easily exceeds $200 billion a year, with the lion's share still going to TV (although Internet advertising is catching up fast). Let's face it, corporate America and the media aren't just in bed together... they're joined at the hip like Siamese twins!

Do you know what it costs today to buy a 30-second spot during the Super Bowl? More than $2.5 million, up from $1 million in 2000. The big traditional companies buy three... four... five of those spots and then pay Cindy Crawford or Tiger Woods. For the six hours leading up to and including the playing of the Super Bowl, advertisers spent a record—now get this—$221 MILLION. Budweiser led all advertisers with 10 spots, costing them more than $20 million for just one afternoon of advertising.

Ever see any ads for a Network Marketing company during the Super Bowl? Not a one. And let's face facts—the media has no love for an industry that doesn't have any major advertising bills to pay... and never will!

NEGATIVE MOTIVATION

Is there a positive side to this flood of negativity the media dumps on Network Marketing? You bet—although I've got to say, I'll be one of the first to rejoice when they begin to praise us instead of trying to cut us down. But let me illustrate the good news resulting from all the bad news with a story.

One day there were two curious frogs who fell into a pail of milk. The pail was pretty deep, so it was a long way up to get out of the pail. The frogs started jumping and jumping, but neither of them could quite reach the top edge of the pail.

It just so happened that one of the frogs was nearly deaf. So he didn't particularly notice at first that some other frogs had gathered at the rim of the pail. They were razzin' and jeerin' at him and his friend. They laughed and pointed at the two stuck in the pail. They mocked them and called them names.

Now the other frog heard all of this and he became pretty angry. He jumped and jumped, just saying to himself, "I'll show those guys—wait 'til I get my hands on them." But after a while, he got tired. He became dejected and bitter, and the more the frogs outside taunted him, the more depressed he became. Finally, he gave up hope, stopped trying to jump out—and drowned.

The other frog—the one who was nearly deaf—didn't hear the negativity of his buddies, and he kept trying and trying to jump out of the pail. Every time he looked up at them, he got even more determined and would jump even higher. Eventually, all of his jumping around turned the milk to butter—and he was able to jump free of the pail with one easy hop.

When he got out, the other frogs asked him why all their name calling and making fun of him hadn't discouraged him like the other frog. The frog replied, "Gee, I had no idea you were puttin' me down. I thought you were cheering me on!"

There are many "hard-of-hearing frogs" in Network Marketing today.

We think the media are just cheering us on.

FREEDOM OF SPEECH—EXCEPT IN NETWORK MARKETING

The very first amendment to the Bill of Rights of the Constitution of the United States of America is our most famous, guaranteeing all citizens freedom of speech.

I quote:

"Congress shall make no law... abridging the freedom of speech...."

Well, I guess a number of states and the Federal Trade Commission (FTC) can "abridge" anyway. I guess the Constitution doesn't apply to them.

You see, you—whoever you are, whatever you do for a living—can stand up anytime, anywhere... in front of any number of people... and tell them how much income you earn—unless you are a Network Marketer.

Check this out. In some states, Network Marketers are not permitted to mention their incomes—I'm talking about their own personal, factual, documented-on-paper-by-the-IRS incomes—in public!

I suppose they are allowed to lock themselves in the bathroom and scream out the numbers on their most recent commission checks until they turn blue. But they cannot announce it to a group of people. If they do, the state attorneys general will invite them to jail and the FTC will—if the numbers are big enough to make it worth their while—swoop down on them like starving legal eagles.

What the state attorneys general say Networkers can do is to take all the money your company paid out in commissions in your local geographic region, divide it by the total number of distributors in that area—both active ones and those who aren't even involved anymore—and you can tell everybody that figure.

It's like forcing a professional athlete like Tiger Woods to state his income only in terms of the average salary of all the professional golfers in the world put together... including all the retired players! Can you imagine that?

I mean, pick any profession—doctors, lawyers, accountants, actors, writers—are they forced to do that? Does the government single them out for a special dose of unconstitutional "abridging the freedom of speech...?" No way!

They wouldn't stand for it. Neither would you.

But for Network Marketers, that's the way it is.

NETWORK MARKETING MONEY—'IT'S JUST TOO MUCH!'

A couple of years ago, *U.S. News and World Report* published a list of the highest-paying occupations in America. They listed the specific career and gave the upper income range.

They refused to print the income for Network Marketers—they said it wasn't believable! Now that's unbelievable! I guess it's true what they say about how the more powerful you are, the bigger your enemies are, too.

Let's say you were sitting atop a glass-and-granite building in New York or Boston and the talk around the big polished conference table was about how come you're not selling more xyz product. And let's say some junior executive (clearly on his way down) had the stupidity to say that Network Marketing was taking a big bite out of your market share—what would you think? What would you do?

Put yourself in their shoes—if you were involved with any of these major companies whose lunch was getting eaten slowly but surely by an upstart industry... an industry that talks to consumers face to face—what would you do?

Remember the rule, "If you can't beat 'em—join 'em"? Well, these traditional companies have their own rule: "If you can't beat 'em—*beat 'em up!*"

IS THERE ANYBODY WHO ISN'T TRYING TO BEAT UP ON NETWORK MARKETING?

Lots of big, traditional companies love Direct Selling companies. Berkshire-Hathaway, the Fortune 500 conglomerate, for one. Warren Buffett, Berkshire's CEO and the second richest man in the world, owns more profitable companies than most men own ties. And he has a special fondness for lean-and-mean Direct Selling companies, which is why he owns three of them among the dozens of companies operating under the Berkshire-Hathaway umbrella.

Citigroup, the biggest, most profitable financial institution in the world, owns a Networking company, as does Time-Warner, Inc., the multi-media giant that also owns *Time* magazine, AOL, HBO, and Warner Brothers movie studio, among others.

These three Fortune 500 companies LOVE their Networking subsidiaries, and for good reason. They're growing and making money and making stockholders very happy.

And you know who else isn't trying to beat up on Network Marketing anymore? Dozens of international companies, such as Dell Computers, Office Depot, Barnes & Noble, FTD Florists, and Sony, to name a few, offering thousands of name-brand products available through Network Marketing.

More and more corporations have stopped trying to beat us—and started joining us. And the tidal wave is just starting to build!

DOLLARS AND SENSE

Why? Because Network Marketing is making more and more common sense—which in business is defined as dollars and cents—the bottom line.

Meanwhile, costs in the conventional marketing world have gone crazy:

- Advertising is too expensive even for multi-million-dollar companies...
- Distribution and sales costs are skyrocketing...
- Thousands of wonderful products that consumers really want never make it to the marketplace because even the biggest companies simply cannot afford the high cost of marketing their products...
- Consumers no longer trust companies or their ads, and retail clerks don't know their left hand from their right as to how to educate and inform shoppers about what they're buying or how to use it...
- Consumers are demanding more for their money...

112

- Consumers are demanding better customer service and shop-at-home convenience...
- And competition is getting tougher and tougher for everyone...

The unconventional approach of Network Marketing has more and more of the right answers—right when businesses need them most.

I know you haven't been told the truth about Network Marketing before.

Now you've got a pretty good idea why.

And you know what? In a way, I'm kinda' glad we haven't been told the truth.

NETWORK MARKETING IS STILL A BEST-KEPT SECRET

It's like finding a great fishing hole. The kind where you throw your line in and—bang!—catch fish in minutes. Then another and another. Big ones, too! It's the kind of discovery you share carefully. It's a secret. You only tell your good friends about it.

Network Marketing is like the gold mine story about a man who was driving along a mountain road late at night when his headlights reflected off something bright on the side of the road.

The man eased his truck onto the shoulder, grabbed his flashlight, and walked over to the bushes where he thought he saw the object.

He parted the bushes and scanned the ground with his flashlight. As he pushed back the final branch, he was astonished to find himself staring at a bar of gold near the opening to a huge cave. He lunged forward and explored the cave with his flashlight. It was filled with gold bars!

The man couldn't believe his good fortune! He grabbed an armful of gold bars and loaded up his truck. But when he came back to the cave, he was even more amazed... magically, there were twice as many gold bars than there were before!

He worked fast and furious and filled his truck so full of gold bars that the tires were ready to burst. By the time he left, the gold bars were spilling out of the cave, through the bushes, and even closer to the road.

He covered the opening to the cave with the bushes as best he could and headed for home.

WHO WOULD YOU SHARE YOUR GOLD WITH?

Now let me ask you. If you were that man, who would you share your gold mine secret with? Would you run an ad in the local newspaper or stop strangers on the street and tell them you had discovered a gold mine? Or would you share your discovery with people you know and care about? Of course you'd tell those people closest to you first, wouldn't you?

I admit it—there's a part of me that thinks Network Marketing is like a gold mine. I mean, I love the idea that average people are turning their lives around—ordinary people living extraordinary lives. It's fine with me if the "corporate fat cats" come to the party—sooner or later. But truthfully, I'm real content to make it later.

Much later.

Make 'em wait and sweat it out.

After all, that's what they've been doing to you and me—for years!

I know they're coming on board the Networking train. Everybody is. It's just a matter of time. But before they do, before Network Marketing gets to be a multi-hundred-billion-dollar industry like franchising, I want all of us "little guys" to get ours first.

The people who've had the American Dream stolen from them should have the first shot. I'm all for letting the new paradigm people get the cake while the old paradigm thieves get the crumbs this time.

What's the song say?

"And the first ones now,
Will later be last.
For the times, they are a-changin'."

Folks, "The answer is blowin' in the wind"—and what a wind!
It's going to be the biggest hurricane in history.
And its name is Network Marketing.

Network
Marketing—
and YOU!

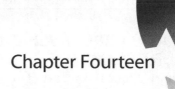

Chapter Fourteen

Are You Riding a Dead Horse?

*The richest people in the world
build networks. Everyone else
is trained to look for work.*
—Robert Kiyosaki
"The Business School"

A friend of mine working for a small private high school handed me an illustrated children's book with this odd title:
If You're Riding a Horse and It Dies, Get Off.

The book is a humorous fable about the need to totally rethink education in this country. The book opens with the drawing of a child riding a horse in front of a one-room schoolhouse. On the next page, the horse dies with the child still sitting in the saddle. On each of the next 17 pages, you see different "experts" weighing in on their opinions as to how to ride a dead horse. Here are a few:

"Let's visit some schools that are successfully riding dead horses."

"Let's assemble a committee to study dead horses."

"I think we should raise the standards for riding dead horses."

On the last two pages, a little boy walks up, points at the horse, and says, "I know what to do! If you're riding a horse and it dies, get off the horse… and try something new." On the opposite page, a shiny, new automobile has replaced the dead horse.

CAN YOUR CURRENT VEHICLE DELIVER YOU TO YOUR DREAMS?

No mystery about the moral of this story, is there? But just in case a reader might miss the moral, the authors spell out the message with these words:

"If you were riding a horse and it died, what would you do? Ancient wisdom advises the rider to dismount and find a better mode of transportation, whether it be another horse or something entirely different. *Unfortunately, too many people try to revive the dead horse with well-intentioned yet unrealistic solutions* [italics mine]."

What about you? Are you riding a dead horse? To find out, answer these questions honestly:

Will your current job take you where you want to go... or is it just a habit?

Are you making progress on your retirement plans... or sitting still?

Are you heading in the direction of your dreams... or stuck in place?

Are you growing in your current occupation... or dying on the vine?

Are you getting paid what you're *really* worth... or just what the job is worth?

Are you getting ahead in your career... or just treading water?

Is your future bright... or are the lights dim and getting dimmer?

One final question: Is your current career a shiny, new vehicle that can deliver you to your dreams in style?... Or is it a dead or dying horse?

NETWORK MARKETING: ALL GASSED UP AND READY TO DRIVE

Robert Kiyosaki, author of the *Rich Dad Poor Dad* book series, has this to say about Network Marketing:

"The Network Marketing industry continues to grow faster than franchises or traditional business. Simply put, Network Marketing, with its low cost of entry and great training programs, is an idea whose time has come."

118

After selling a successful traditional business and investing wisely in real estate, Kiyosaki was able to retire at age 47. Obviously, he knows a thing or two about creating financial freedom, as evidenced by his 10 bestselling books detailing how to create wealth by converting earned income into passive income.

What is it about Network Marketing that compels super-successful businessmen—like Robert Kiyosaki and Warren Buffett—to sing its praises and, in Buffett's case, to buy three Direct Selling companies?

To answer that, let's look at the special features that set Network Marketing apart from traditional businesses and make it, to use Kiyosaki's words, "an idea whose time has come." And, according to the experts, is just getting ramped up for blast off.

NETWORK MARKETING: OPPORTUNITY OF A LIFETIME

We've already talked about how every organization is shaped like a pyramid, including our military, the government, the Boy Scouts, and even your church. And we distinguished between legal pyramids and illegal pyramids, concluding that pyramids are legal as long as value flows down from the top (in the form of products or services) in exchange for money flowing up from the bottom. Which means, by definition, the vast majority of Network Marketing companies are legal. (The ones that aren't legal don't stay in business long 'cause their founders end up in the calaboose sharing a cell with the Enron crooks!).

So far, so good.

But just because a business enterprise is legal doesn't necessarily mean it's a great opportunity. I mean, mowing the neighbor's lawn and hosting a car wash are both legal business enterprises, but I wouldn't consider either a great business opportunity.

So, why do I say Network Marketing is the average person's best opportunity for making money while making a difference in people's lives? Lots of reasons. Off the top of my head, here are the 20 biggest reasons for people who are riding a dead horse to dismount and jump in the driver's seat of the super-charged, dream-fueled vehicle known as Network Marketing.

20 ADVANTAGES OF OWNING A NETWORK MARKETING BUSINESS

1. **Franchise-Like Business Model:** Often called a "personal franchise" or "alternative franchise," Networking takes the best of franchising—a proven, duplicatable business model... and eliminates the worst of franchising—enormous up-front franchising fees and monthly percentage of profits paid back to the parent company. Ugh!

2. **Grows Exponentially:** Most businesses grow *linearly by addition*—one store plus a second store plus a third, etc. Networking grows *exponentially by multiplication*—you get six new people... who each get six new people... who each get six new people, etc.

3. **Leverage Time & Money:** Leverage is best summed up by J. Paul Getty's axiom, "I'd rather have 1% of 100 men's efforts than 100% of my own." The key to big profits in Networking isn't for one super salesman to move a ton of product, but for lots of average people each to move a little bit of product, month in and month out.

4. **Average Person's Best Chance to Earn Above-Average Income:** Network Marketing doesn't require expensive specialized college degrees—just an open mind and a willingness to learn a unique system of distribution.

5. **System of Education & Training:** Systems are proven procedures that people can learn and copy to get the most out of their ability. Great Networkers have a system they can plug their new people into.

6: **Recurring Income:** As an employee, you trade time for dollars—one hour of work equals one hour of income. With Network Marketing, you can leverage your time and efforts, creating income that keeps coming in even during your off hours.

7. **Help Others While Helping Yourself:** What better way to make your mark in life than by giving back to others? The best way to get everything you want out of life is to help others get what they want.

8. **Low Cost of Entry, High-Profit Potential:** In Networking, you can start a potentially high-profit "personal franchise" for hundreds of dollars, as opposed to spending hundreds of thousands of dollars (or more) to start a traditional franchise.

120

9. **Choose the People You Work With:** In Networking, you select your teammates, as opposed to a job where you are thrown in with strangers, many of whom you would NEVER choose as friends.

10. **Be Your Own Boss:** Set your own hours... set your own goals... choose your own projects... work 2 hours a day or 20 hours a day. You're the CEO of your own company, so you call the shots, and you reap the rewards.

11. **Choose Level of Participation:** Need a few hundred extra dollars a month for spending money? How about a part-time opportunity? Or a full-time career? Want to stay local? Or expand internationally? The choice is yours and yours alone.

12. **No Glass Ceiling:** Tired of banging your head against corporate cultures that hold you back for no other reason than your gender?... Or ethnic background?... Or accent?... Or failure to attend the "right" school? Networking is totally democratic—whoever gets results, gets money and recognition. Period!

13. **No Cap on Your Income:** In a job, the owner pays you at wholesale and then sells your services in the marketplace for retail and pockets the difference. Consequently, you'll never make more than what the job is worth. In Networking, the sky is the limit.

14. **Unlimited Territory:** Traditional franchises restrict your territory to an area of town. Not so in a "personal franchise." Wherever the parent company has a presence, you can have a growing organization.

15. **Low Overhead, Little Inventory:** In Network Marketing, many multi-million-dollar earners work out of a home office, preferring to put their profits in their pockets instead of offices and employees.

16. **Get Paid to Pull People Up:** Network Marketing gives people a personal *hand up* (as opposed to a government *hand out*) motivating them to grow and become self reliant and independent.

17. **Buy Products at Wholesale for Personal Use:** Because Network Marketing offers exclusive, cutting-edge products unavailable in retail stores, distributors enjoy the added advantage of receiving discounts and rebates on one-of-a-kind products for personal and family use.

18. **Exploits e-commerce:** Historically, Networking companies and their leading distributors have been early adopters of

technology. Little wonder, then, that most Networking companies have set up content-rich e-commerce sites that make ordering easy and convenient while offering ongoing education and training for the distributor base.

19: **Encourages Personal Growth:** Companies and successful distributors understand that to grow your business, you must first grow yourself. Which is why they recommend and produce books, tapes, and tools that encourage people to dream big dreams and then make them come true by growing themselves and their businesses to their fullest potential.

20: **Have Fun, Make Friends, Make Money, Make a Difference:** The best thing about Network Marketing isn't that people are getting rich (although many are), it's that people are *building rich lives* in the process. Making money is nice, but having fun, making friends, and making a difference—priceless!

There you have it—20 reasons why Network Marketing is a new and better way of working and living.

Truly, this is an industry whose time has come. Right now experts estimate that Direct Selling, led by Network Marketing, is a $100 billion—yes BILLION with a "B"—a year business... yet, amazingly, it's still in its infancy! King Kong in diapers!

To learn where the industry is heading in the coming decades, turn to the next chapter: "Why Network Marketing Is Exploding!"

Chapter Fifteen

Why Network Marketing Is Exploding!

What is more mortifying than
to feel you have missed
the plum for lack of courage
to shake the tree?
—Logan Smith
"Afterthoughts"

Throughout this book, we've pointed out how times have changed and how they'll be changing even faster tomorrow. We've pointed out how technology is marching—more correctly, racing—forward, making entire industries and ways of working obsolete almost overnight.

It's because of technology that Network Marketing is exploding!

Before the computer, no Network Marketing company could grow any bigger than their ability to keep track of their distributors. Imagine having to take and process orders, keep track of individual network organizations, and issue timely and accurate commission checks for 10,000... or even 100,000—distributors. Impossible!

Not anymore, thanks to computer technology.

IN FRONT OF THE TECHNOLOGY CURVE

It's hard to imagine Network Marketing without credit cards, airplanes that fly coast to coast in less than six hours, free long distance phone service, unlimited hours on cell phones, PDAs, voice mail, e-mail, instant messaging, phone calls over the Internet, pod-casting, toll-free phone numbers, teleconferencing, etc.

With one click of a computer key, Network Marketers today can send product and training information anywhere in the world in an instant. They can prospect for new partners on their car phones—while stuck in traffic. A thousand people or more can get on a weekly teleconference call or view a live video broadcast on the Internet and invite new people to hear all about the company's products and opportunity, without leaving their own living rooms!

Today Network Marketers can tell people across the country (or around the world, for that matter) about their company, products, and income opportunity by sending them CDs or DVDs... or by having them log onto a Website. Talk about convenience—for just a few dollars your new distributors can receive trainings from the top producers in the industry. Or they can tune in to a live satellite program broadcast right into their homes.

None of this was possible 20 years ago—even 5 years ago, for that matter—because much of the technology wasn't available or affordable until recently. And tomorrow's technology will be even more extraordinary. With the growing popularity of the Internet, the possibilities for the future are virtually endless!

Networkers have always been early adapters of communication technology, so rest assured, as soon as a leading-edge product hits the market, industry leaders will adapt it to their business.

YOU AIN'T SEEN NOTHIN' YET!

Imagine selecting the Network Marketing products you want from a full-color talking catalog on your home computer in the kitchen... imagine ordering what you want simply by touching the screen... imagine having conference calls via video phone... imagine having multi-media video presentations sent directly to your home by satellite whenever you want... imagine talking back to your computer or TV with interactive programming... imagine having your monthly commission checks automatically and instantly transferred to your electronic checking account.

The extraordinary advance of technology is opening up vast horizons of possibility for Network Marketing—and it's happening right now. That's why Network Marketing is just coming into its own. Futurist Faith Popcorn says it best:

> "Network Marketing is the wave of the future. As the person-to-person deliverers get classier and better and more trusted, everything will be sold person to person and inter-actively on TV. I think the problem is the retail environment is simply going to have to close the doors. Nobody wants to go there. And Network Marketing has the solution."

HARD TIMES—TOUGH CHOICES

We've talked about the reality of the most productive time in this nation's history, yet a time when millions of people will be changing jobs—or even careers... a time of 20% unemployment (or 80% underemployment) in many industrialized countries!

We've talked about the American Dream of health, happiness, security, and freedom... and how fewer and fewer people are in a position to have even one or two of these qualities in their lives, much less all of them.

We've talked about how the odds are stacked against us in the working world today... about glass ceilings, "unequal opportunity," the sand trap of using a college education to lead to a corporate career track, and the scams and schemes that rip off almost any chance we have for getting to the top and living the good life.

We've talked about the lack of real creativity and control in the workplace... and the lack of satisfaction and fulfillment available in most conventional jobs.

We've discussed illegal and legal pyramid schemes and how they're sucking the life out of the average American woman and man.

We've talked about how frustrated people are... how angry people are at what's happening... and how millions of people are feeling totally powerless to do anything about it.

What we've shown—sadly—is that for most of us, the future can be a pretty hopeless situation.

125

Remember the definition of hope? "Hope is the expectation that someone, or something, will come along and save you."

My friends, the cavalry ain't coming to save you. That bugle you hear isn't playing a cavalry charge... its playing taps for the dear departed jobs being outsourced to India and China. Sure, you always have the hope of hitting the lottery. But things are pretty hopeless when all that's left of the American Dream is a one-in-a-zillion chance to make it big.

That's not the American Dream. That's the American fantasy. Difference is, dreams can come true.

DREAMING OF SUCCESS

Let me tell you a wonderful story that illustrates the biggest key to success.

One day, a man walked into a psychiatrist's office and boy, did he look bad! He was ashen gray—like death warmed over—and he was shaking all over. His eyes were sunk deep into his head. He hadn't slept in months! He begged the doctor to help him!

The man told the psychiatrist about a recurring dream he'd been having. Seems that every time he'd fall asleep, he'd have the same frightening nightmare. There he was, just walking down the street. He'd go right up to this building... come up to this huge door—and then, no matter how hard he pushed—he could never open the door to get inside!

He'd push and strain against the door—nothing! It wouldn't budge an inch. No matter what near-superhuman strength he could muster—nothing. The door just wouldn't open!

He would wake up in a cold sweat, shaking—scared and exhausted. He dreaded the dream so much that no matter how tired he became, he was afraid to close his eyes. He said it felt like he was going to die if he didn't get in that door—but it just wouldn't open!

The doctor asked him why it was so important to open that door, and the man replied that it was the door to his future. This was the door that would lead from failure to success, and he couldn't open it!

The psychiatrist thought for a moment, then asked, "You have this dream every time you sleep?"

126

The man nodded yes. The doctor thought long and hard—and then smiled.

"I think I have the cure for your nightmare," the doctor said. "Tonight, before you close your eyes, I want you to tell yourself that when you come to the door again, you're going to notice everything about it, every detail, no matter how insignificant you think it is. Then come back tomorrow, and tell me what you've seen."

When the doctor saw the man the next day, he couldn't believe his eyes! Gone was the shaken, shrunken fellow who was there the day before. This man looked vibrant and alive. His eyes were bright, and he was smiling! The startled psychiatrist quickly ushered the man into his office for an explanation.

"I followed the advice you gave me," the patient said excitedly, "and before I fell off to sleep, I told myself to notice and remember every detail about the door to success.

"Just like always, the dream returned as soon as I nodded off. When I came up to the door, I pushed harder than I ever had before. I strained against it—pushing and pushing. Like always, nothing happened. Finally, I remembered your advice, and I stepped back and studied every detail of the door. And do you know what I saw?"

"No," said the doctor, excitedly. "Tell me, tell me."

"There was a sign on the door I'd been pushing," the man said, smiling.

"The sign said, 'PULL!'"

ARE YOU PUSHING—OR PULLING—ON THE DOOR TO SUCCESS?

Are you straining to get ahead in life, struggling against the odds, pushing to get ahead, only to find yourself locked out—stuck in a dead-end rut with no way out?

Well, quit pushing!

Pull!

The door to the future—the door to the American Dream—is wide open for you. There's no struggle involved… no nightmare of fear. All you have to do is what the *Bible* tells you:

"Ask, and it shall be given you; seek and you shall find; knock, and it shall be opened unto you."

That is, if it's the door to Network Marketing.

As you've seen throughout this book—and more importantly, in your own experience—all doors do not lead to the future you desire.

Network Marketing can and does.

Millions of people have passed through Network Marketing's door to a richer, more rewarding life. They've learned from direct experience how they can have their cake and eat it, too.

Today these people own businesses of their own. Thanks to Network Marketing, they're the boss, the CEO of their own growing enterprise—working when they choose, where they choose, with whom they choose.

Network Marketers choose whether they work part-time or full-time, and many who began just to supplement their incomes have made Network Marketing their full-time career.

Network Marketers have learned the power of leverage, what J. Paul Getty meant when he said, "I'd rather have 1% of 100 people's efforts than 100% of my own." They've seen how a lot of people doing a little bit each can keep all the qualities of "small is beautiful," and yet, accomplish a big, BIG job.

They've experienced—or have begun to experience—going beyond mere security to true financial freedom: having all the money they need... doing what they want, when they want... with no one to tell them otherwise.

You know, 80% of all bankruptcies would be prevented if people had as little as an extra $500 per month! In Network Marketing thousands and thousands of people have that—and thousands more have 10, 20, 100 times that—and more!

And it's not just about money, either. It's about running your own show... calling your own shots... doing well for yourself while doing good for others... and sharing your dreams and your time with the people who count the most in your life—your family and friends.

'I CAN'T SEE MYSELF IN NETWORK MARKETING'
People tell me that all the time.

"I'm a doctor... I'm a lawyer... an engineer... an accountant... a printer... a teacher... I just can't see myself in Network Marketing," they say.

When they tell me that, here's what I say:

"That's interesting. You see, I was going to offer you an opportunity with one of my companies driving a garbage truck. Would you be interested in the job?"

And the answer always is, "Are you nuts!?! NO—I don't want to drive a garbage truck!"

Then I respond with, "Okay, then, I've got another job that pays a million dollars a year! You'd be perfect for the position. Are you interested in that opportunity?"

"Absolutely!" they answer. "What's the job?"

"It's driving a garbage truck," I tell them.

One guy summed it all up when he said, "Oh, that's different. That's business!"

Well, Network Marketing is different, too. It's business. BIG business—and it's not driving a garbage truck, I can tell you that! (And if you're real successful, you'll be driving a Lexus or a BMW, not a garbage truck).

You can either make up your mind right now that you won't have anything to do with Networking—or, you can open up your mind and take advantage of an industry whose time has come.

Just think—what if it actually did provide you with the perfect vehicle for getting all you want out of life?

Can you afford to pass up that possibility?

TAKING A CHANCE ON CHANGE

You know, sometimes change is a difficult thing to accept. I know. When I was building boats for $5.50 an hour or waiting tables for $150 a week, I agonized for months about whether or not I should quit my job—a job I absolutely hated!—and risk getting out of my comfort zone by trying something different.

President John Kennedy once said:

"Change is the law of life. And those who look only to the past or the present are certain to miss the future."

129

He couldn't have been more right!

Just think: 40 years ago only 6% of meals were eaten out of the home (today, 60% are eaten out)... 25 years ago there were no video stores... less than 20 years ago Russia was a communist country... and 10 years ago only computer nerds were plugged into the Internet!

The lesson is clear: Change—or get left behind.

ASK YOURSELF THESE QUESTIONS:
• Am I truly happy with my current job?
  • Am I making all the money I deserve?
  • Do I have the time I want for my family... for my friends... for myself?
  • Am I helping others while I help myself?
  • Am I growing and developing personally at the rate I want?
  • Am I in control of my own work—my life... or is someone or something pulling my strings?
  • Am I willing to do what it takes to have the American Dream?

Several years ago I asked myself these same questions—and I didn't like the answers at all!

So I changed. I opened up... took a look... and took the biggest step of my life!

I quit pushing and PULLED!

I challenge you to do the same.

I challenge you to ask yourself the toughest questions of all. And if you don't like your answers—like I didn't like mine—then do what I did. Take advantage of Network Marketing now before it's too late.

WHY NOW IS THE BEST TIME TO GET INVOLVED
We've all heard the expression, "Timing is everything in life and business."

The key to running a successful business... or to getting rich... is to get in at the right time... to get in on a business explosion just before the boom... to catch a wave just as it starts to rise.

There are four phases of growth in the cycle of any successful business or industry. First is the **Foundation Phase**. Next, the

130

Concentration Phase. Then comes the **Momentum Phase**. And last, the **Stability Phase**.

You could call the Foundation Phase the "pioneering years." The industry is just getting started, and the general public doesn't understand what you're doing because it's "new" and "unproven." The pioneering years are tough. Lots of rejection... lots of ups and downs while the foundation is being laid. These are the high-risk years.

It's like the pioneers who settled the West. Because they were the first ones to open up the frontier, they had the first shot at the best land. But they were also the ones who got the arrows in their backs!

The Foundation Phase for Network Marketing started in the late 1940s and lasted until 1979, when Amway won a landmark court decision against the FTC. This decision made it clear—once and for all—that Network Marketing was a legal, legitimate system for selling products and services.

After the pioneering years comes the Concentration Phase. This is when business starts to shift gears, to gain some acceptance from the masses. When the first McDonald's restaurant opened up, for example, it was little more than a local curiosity. No one but the founder, Ray Kroc, believed it was the beginning of an American institution. By the time the 100th McDonald's opened up, however, this trend-setting franchise was not only gaining acceptance... it was generating lots of excitement.

CRITICAL MASS: HEADED FOR TAKEOFF!

Today Network Marketing is at the final stage of the Concentration Phase... and entering the explosive Momentum Phase! The entire industry is just about to undergo a dynamic phenomenon called Critical Mass. When an industry hits Critical Mass, something magical happens. It's as if someone pushes a cultural button, and voilá!—everybody wants what you've got. Critical Mass means the products and method of distribution have gained popular acceptance, and they become market driven. When Critical Mass hits, growth goes into overdrive... and sales begin to explode!

Think about this: In the 1960s, personal computers didn't even exist. In the '70s, only "techies" owned them. But by the mid-'80s, the industry hit Critical Mass... and today, almost 75% of the homes in North America have a personal computer! The same happened to dishwashers. And microwaves. And cell phones. And CD players. And DVD players. And digital cameras. And the Internet. Once they hit Critical Mass—BOOM... demand mushroomed and sales went through the roof!

GET IN... AND BUCKLE UP!

The entire Network Marketing industry is just starting to enter Critical Mass... which means the first two decades of the 21st century will be a period of tremendous growth... of tremendous opportunity... and of tremendous profits!

Just think—thousands of North Americans have made fortunes in Network Marketing by building their businesses in the U.S. and Canada. Can you imagine the fortunes that will be made when Networking reaches Critical Mass in Malaysia... Russia... China... and India? That's like adding the population of 10 more USAs as your potential partners. When that happens, this industry will explode into a multi-trillion-dollar-a-year business... which means the top distributors won't just be millionaires—they'll be billionaires!

That's why you've got to position yourself in this industry today! There has never been a better time to start laying the foundation to your international business!

Right now it's projected that only 2% of the population is involved in Networking. But I predict that figure will soon jump to 10%! Which means the vast majority of the money to be made in this industry will likely be made in the coming years!

ARE YOU ONE OF THE NEXT MILLIONAIRES?

In his latest book, *The Next Millionaires*, bestselling author and noted economist Paul Zane Pilzer observes that from 1991 to 2001, the number of millionaires in the U.S. doubled from 3.6 million to 7.2 million.

According to Pilzer, this wealth-building trend will continue for the next decade, more than doubling again to nearly 20 million millionaires before 2020.

Where will the next millionaires come from?

132

Pilzer's answer is home-based businesses, led by Network Marketers, the "new entrepreneurs" distributing education, knowledge, and opportunity along with leading-edge products and services.

In Pilzer's words, "Today we are poised for an economic growth spurt that will far exceed the explosion of the 1990s, and those entering the growth industry of Direct Selling are perfectly positioned to benefit from the boom ahead."

TAKE A CHANCE ON YOU!

You couldn't pick a better time to get involved in Network Marketing! In the next few years, average people just like you—perhaps someone in your neighborhood or someone you see at church each Sunday—will make a ton of money in Network Marketing by taking advantage of Critical Mass.

Never before in history have so many people been in a position to take advantage of such an explosive mega-trend. That's what makes Network Marketing so exciting... and fantastic! When Network Marketing reaches Critical Mass and explodes all over the world, more people—more average men and women—will grab a piece of the money pie than during any other movement or opportunity in the history of the world!

The risk is small. The reward is great. And there will never, ever be a better time to get involved than right now!

So go ahead... do what I did and take a chance on an industry whose time has come. Better yet, take a chance on yourself!

I dare you to pull when the rest of the world is pushing.

I dare you to be different... to dream.

But most of all, I dare you to become one of the 10 million millionaires in the decade ahead—and claim your fair share of the American Dream!